CLEAN EATING
INSTANT POT
COOKBOOK

CLEAN EATING
INSTANT POT COOKBOOK

80 Healthy Recipes for Busy People

Lauren Keating

Photography by Laura Flippen

ROCKRIDGE
PRESS

For general information on our other products and services or to obtain technical support, please contact our Customer Care Department within the United States at (866) 744-2665, or outside the United States at (510) 253-0500.

Rockridge Press publishes its books in a variety of electronic and print formats. Some content that appears in print may not be available in electronic books, and vice versa.

Interior and Cover Designer: Linda Snorina
Art Producer: Samantha Ulban
Editor: Reina Glenn
Production Editor: Ruth Sakata Corley
Production Manager: Riley Hoffman

Photography © 2021 Laura Flippen. Food styling by Laura Flippen.

Cover: Seafood Cioppino, page 71.

ISBN: Print 978-1-64876-455-4
eBook 978-1-64876-456-1

R0

Contents

Introduction

I first started dabbling in the world of clean eating in my early twenties.

After trying and failing at several popular diets, I finally found what worked best for me: limiting processed food and refined carbs and eating lots of fresh, in-season fruits and vegetables, lean proteins, and whole grains. I stabilized my weight without obsessively counting calories or carbs, I had more energy, and—the most exciting part—the food tasted way better than any "diet" food ever did. I didn't know then that this lifestyle had a name, but I knew I loved it.

Clean eating is a framework that allows you to enjoy a wide variety of foods, from classic homestyle recipes such as spaghetti and meatballs to international favorites like curries and stir-fries. You can even make clean eating versions of baked goods such as banana bread and lemon bars.

Whenever I fall into a cycle of eating too many processed foods or restaurant meals, I turn back to these nourishing, whole food meals that I know will make my body feel better.

That said, cooking and eating clean takes some planning. I love to cook, but like so many of you, I have a demanding job and a packed calendar that doesn't leave much time to play around in the kitchen—especially on weeknights. That's why I love my Instant Pot so much. It helps get delicious, nutritious meals on the table quickly with the least effort possible.

Whether you're looking to fully commit to a clean eating lifestyle or just add a few healthy recipes to your arsenal, you'll find exactly what you need in the pages of this book.

Chapter 1

Clean Eating Made Simple

Thanks to the Instant Pot, cooking healthy, whole food meals has never been easier. In this chapter, we'll go over what clean eating means and why the Instant Pot is such a fantastic tool when following a clean eating lifestyle.

If you're new to the Instant Pot, don't worry. We'll also cover the basics of how to use your pressure cooker and what to do if things go wrong.

Why Clean Eating and the Instant Pot Are a Perfect Match

What is clean eating, anyway? There are lots of variations of clean eating, but simply put, it means avoiding processed foods and focusing on whole, nutrient-dense foods that nourish your body. It's not a diet but rather a way of eating that ensures you don't need to go on a diet ever again.

You might have learned about the four food groups or the food pyramid back in elementary school. If a food fits neatly into one of those categories, there's a good chance it's suitable for a whole foods diet.

Many people dip their toes into the world of clean eating because they're looking to lose weight, but this lifestyle can help with so much more than that. Focusing on clean eating means developing a healthy relationship with food and giving your body nourishment so it can perform at its best. You don't need to count calories, restrict food groups, fast, or take any other dramatic steps associated with most popular diets. In fact, you can follow a clean eating lifestyle without a weight loss goal at all. Personally, I like this way of eating because it leaves me feeling recharged. I also notice a dramatic improvement in my hair and skin when I focus on eating nourishing whole foods.

In today's super-busy world, where takeout meals and prepared foods just seem easier than cooking a meal from scratch, clean eating can feel impossible. But once you get into the groove, it will become second nature—and your body will thank you for it.

Instant Pots have made clean eating easier than ever. Their main appeal is speed. Whole grains and hard winter squashes cook quickly under pressure, and it's possible to have a healthy meal on the table in less than 30 minutes. But when it comes to health, Instant Pots have even more benefits. Pressure cookers cook foods quickly and evenly, helping them retain up to 90 percent of their water-soluble vitamins. That means your food is more nutritious! The airtight environment also retains more moisture, making it well suited for cooking foods without added fats or sugar.

Before learning about the best ways to use an Instant Pot to cook healthy recipes, it's important to understand the foods that will form the backbone of the clean eating lifestyle. So, let's dive in!

THE BENEFITS OF CLEAN EATING

Eating nourishing whole foods is linked to a wide range of short- and long-term health benefits, from stabilizing blood sugar and improving digestion to increasing energy and improving mood. It's also better for the planet. Here are just a few benefits that you can look forward to.

Weight management: Excess water weight and bloating are linked to processed foods that are full of sodium. Focusing on vegetables and whole grains will help build lean muscle and reduce inflammation. Eating this way, you'll also have fewer cravings, helping you naturally eat the perfect amount to fuel your body—all without counting calories.

More energy: High-fiber fruits and vegetables take longer to digest than processed foods, helping stabilize your blood sugar and avoid that afternoon crash. Improved digestion can also help you sleep better at night so you wake up refreshed and ready to go.

Better mood: Eating balanced meals high in omega-3s and selenium help boost serotonin levels and keep your spirits high. Plus, you'll have so many delicious foods to get excited about eating!

Improved gut health: Gut health has been a hot topic for the last few years. A diet rich in whole foods and fermented foods such as yogurt and sauerkraut provides a combination of probiotics and prebiotics that help good bacteria in your gut thrive while fighting harmful bacteria and viruses. Consuming more fiber and less processed sugar also helps reduce inflammation in the gut.

Better-tasting food: Slowing down and savoring your meals will help you build a better relationship with your food. Once your taste buds get used to the natural flavors of whole foods, you'll notice the extreme levels of salt and sugar in their processed counterparts (and you may find them less appealing).

Benefits for the planet: Food travels long distances from farm to consumer, and a huge amount of energy is required to process, transport, and package convenience foods. By eating whole foods and supporting your local farm stand, you can reduce your carbon footprint.

Clean Eating Fundamentals

As you begin to focus on healthier eating habits, you'll need to adjust your approach to grocery shopping and meal planning.

Depending on your current eating habits and health goals, this could mean anything from a few simple tweaks to a complete overhaul of your diet. This book has plenty of recipes to get you started, but for long-term success, it's important to understand the nutritional framework of a clean eating lifestyle: the foods that will leave you feeling happy, healthy, and satisfied.

Buy Quality Food

The first rule of clean eating is to buy the best-quality food that you can easily afford. This means emphasizing fruits and vegetables and purchasing high-quality meat, fish, and dairy products that are raised without antibiotics or added hormones. By focusing on ingredients that are as close to their original state in nature as possible, you'll reward your body with maximum nutrition.

I also make an effort to buy local, in-season products from farmers' markets whenever possible. The food tends to be more affordable, and because it hasn't traveled as far and is generally fresher, it tastes better than what you can find at the supermarket. Plus, you can feel good about supporting farmers in your own community.

Many people choose organic food as a way of avoiding added chemicals. Although this is a great goal, buying organic definitely isn't required for clean eating. If you're looking to make informed choices, check out the Environmental Working Group's yearly "Clean 15" and "Dirty Dozen" lists, which categorize produce items based on the amount of pesticide residue commonly found on them (see Resources on page 125).

Limit Sugar and Salt

According to recent studies from both Johns Hopkins and Harvard universities, excess sugar can impact your weight and increase your risk for cardiovascular disease, and too much sodium can contribute to high blood pressure, heart disease, and stroke.

Luckily, your sugar and salt intake will naturally decrease as you minimize the number of processed foods you eat. But be sure to check labels carefully, because even foods that seem healthy can often have unexpected ingredients.

Sugar is often added to store-bought pasta sauce, applesauce, and salad dressing. Seek out unsweetened versions or those sweetened naturally with honey, maple syrup, or dates, or make your own. Sugar is also commonly added to low-fat dairy products to make up for the taste and texture that's lost when removing the fat. Fat is an important nutrient that helps fuel your body and make you feel full, so don't be afraid to include it in moderation in your diet.

Sodium is used as a preservative in canned foods, frozen meals, cured meats, butters, breads, and cheeses. Again, check labels and opt for nitrate-free and low-sodium versions of these foods. Rinsing canned ingredients such as beans can also reduce the sodium content by up to 30 percent.

Eat Balanced Meals

Your body needs both macronutrients and micronutrients to function properly, so it's important to balance your meals and make sure you're getting enough of each.

Macronutrients (carbohydrates, protein, and fats) fuel your body and are needed in larger quantities. Micronutrients (vitamins and minerals) are needed in smaller quantities but are still vitally important for warding off disease and ensuring a strong central nervous system.

To strike the right balance, practice including a fruit or vegetable, lean protein, and healthy fat in every meal you eat. When it comes to fruits and vegetables, try to eat a variety of colors. Yellow and red vegetables are just as important as leafy green ones.

Mind Your Portions

Although the clean eating lifestyle affords a lot of freedom in terms of the types of foods you can enjoy, it's important to remember that these foods still have calories. Portion control is important to staying in good health.

As a general rule of thumb, your meals should be made up of one-quarter lean protein, one-quarter fiber-rich carbohydrate, and one-half nonstarchy vegetables. This is called the balanced plate ratio. You may need to make additional considerations if you follow a special diet, have food allergies, or live with medical conditions such as diabetes or celiac, so be sure to consult with your physician.

If you find yourself getting hungry between meals, try eating five small meals per day instead of three large ones. Or, you could try eating three meals and two balanced snacks. This can help stabilize your blood sugar and keep you satiated.

Stay Hydrated

Staying hydrated regulates your body temperature, reduces brain fog and mood swings, and keeps your joints lubricated. It's also easy to mistake thirst for hunger, so drinking plenty of water throughout the day can help you stay satisfied. Aim to drink ½ to 1 fluid ounce of liquids for every pound of your body weight per day.

In addition to water, choose seltzer or unsweetened teas and coffees. You can also enjoy 100 percent fruit juices in moderation, but be aware of their high sugar content. Avoid high-calorie sweetened drinks like fancy coffees, sodas, and energy drinks, even when they're made with whole food ingredients.

Keep Moving

Clean eating and exercise often build on each other. When you focus on eating nutritious foods, you'll have more energy, and when you make it a habit to exercise, you'll often be motivated to enjoy healthier foods.

Exercise also builds muscle and keeps your heart, lungs, and bones healthy and strong. Exercise also benefits your brain, keeping your energy levels high and your mood balanced.

Now, that's not to say you need to become a gym rat if that's not your style. Just make it a point to move your body in a way that you enjoy for about 20 minutes per day. Personally, I love hiking, dancing, and spinning, although on many days, all I have time for is an after-dinner walk.

WHAT ARE SUPERFOODS?

You'll often hear the word "superfoods" being used by people who focus on a healthy diet. But what exactly are they?

Although there aren't set criteria for something to be labeled a superfood, these foods are often nutrient dense and contain antioxidants, healthy fats, or vitamins. They're also some of the most delicious foods out there, thanks to their naturally occurring phytochemicals, which are responsible for their rich colors and smells.

Some superfoods tend to be expensive, but you can save money by looking for in-season items at your local farmers' market, buying dried items such as beans and nuts in bulk, and purchasing frozen foods.

The following list is made up of popular superfoods worth seeking out as you start your clean eating journey. They're some of my favorite ingredients, and you'll see them frequently in the recipes throughout this book.

- Beans, all kinds

- Berries, all kinds

- Broccoli

- Dark, leafy greens, such as kale, chard, or spinach

- Dark chocolate

- Garlic

- Lentils

- Nuts and seeds, all kinds

- Olive oil

- Salmon and other fatty fish, such as trout or sardines

- Sweet potatoes

- Tea (black, green, and white)

- Tomatoes

- Turmeric, cinnamon, and other warm spices such as star anise and ginger

- Whole grains, all kinds

6 Tips for Making the Transition to Clean Eating

As with any new health regimen, you might face some challenges after you make a commitment to clean eating. Here are some tips to make the transition easier.

1. **Pack your lunch.** Preparing your own meals gives you more control over the quality of food you eat. You might be able to find prepared, healthy, clean eating options, but they tend to be expensive, especially if you don't want to eat salad every day.

2. **Plan ahead.** Planning a weekly menu takes the guesswork out of dinnertime and removes the impulse to order takeout when you're hungry and don't know what to make. You'll also have delicious meals to look forward to! If you're feeling ambitious, you can also prep your meals in advance and store them in the refrigerator or freezer to enjoy throughout the week.

3. **Read nutrition labels.** One benefit of eating whole foods is not having to worry about nutrition labels, but some minimally processed items, such as peanut butter or pasta sauce, require a bit of attention. Get into the habit of reading labels to learn which brands contain only whole, natural ingredients and which have sugar, artificial flavors, dyes, or preservatives. Some common ingredients to avoid include BHA, sodium nitrate, calcium sorbate, BHT, FD&C Red No. 3, tartrazine, and "artificial flavor." When in doubt, buy products with ingredients that you recognize.

4. **Listen to your body.** Pay attention to your body's fullness and hunger cues. Eat when you're hungry and stop when you're full. You can always save your leftovers for later. Avoid mindless eating while watching TV or driving, which can cause you to miss your body's natural cues. When you focus on what you're eating, you'll enjoy the flavors of your food even more.

5. **Stick to the perimeter.** For the most part, you'll find healthy items such as produce, meat, and dairy around the perimeter of the grocery store. The aisles in the center of the store generally contain more processed foods that you'll want to avoid.

6. **Don't deprive yourself.** Focus on all the delicious foods you can eat, not on what you're giving up. Remember that clean eating isn't a fad diet

or a quick fix. This is about nourishing your body for the long term. Don't be afraid to indulge in a healthy version of your favorite treats from time to time. In fact, this book has a whole chapter of desserts (see page 103) that are so delicious you'll have a hard time believing they're healthy!

Getting to Know the Pot

If you've never cooked with an electric pressure cooker before, there will be a slight learning curve as you get used to it. But I promise you'll be a pro in no time, and once you've tried a few recipes from this book, using your Instant Pot will be second nature. Note that all the recipes in this book were developed using the 6-quart Instant Pot DUO, which is considered by many people to be the standard Instant Pot. The recipes will work with any model (all have the same basic functions that are used in these recipes), but you might need to make some minor adjustments depending on the size of your Instant Pot (see "Adjusting for Different Pot Sizes," page 13).

Before you dive in, take a few minutes to familiarize yourself with the various parts, functions, and terminology that you'll likely encounter.

Parts

When you unpack your Instant Pot from its box, you might be surprised by how many components it has. These are different from a lot of other kitchen appliances, but they might be familiar to you if you have experience with traditional stove top pressure cookers. Here is an overview of the Instant Pot's key parts. Be aware that, depending on the model of your pot, the power cord may arrive detached, and there might be other accessories like a measuring cup or spoon in the box.

Base unit: The base unit contains the heating element in the bottom and features a control panel on the front. You'll insert the inner pot into the base unit.

Condensation collector: This is a small, clear cup that attaches to the back of your Instant Pot and collects any moisture that builds up on the pot's rim. This can happen during the cooking process or if the lid is propped open.

Float valve: This valve, located on the pot's lid, regulates the pressure inside the pot.

Inner pot: For most recipes, food will cook directly inside the inner pot. Always double-check to make sure the pot has been returned to the base unit before adding your recipe ingredients; you should never place food directly into the base.

Lid: When cooking under pressure, the lid will lock in place, and you won't be able to remove it until the pressure is released.

Metal trivet: This trivet is used to elevate some foods above the cooking liquid. This is necessary when you want foods to steam instead of boil and, in some cases, to prevent the burn warning from showing up on the Instant Pot's display.

Sealing ring: The silicone sealing ring is a very important part of your Instant Pot; without it, steam will escape, and the pot won't come to pressure. Be sure it's pushed in firmly and no pieces are sticking out from behind the wire.

Steam release handle: Located on the top of the pot's lid, this handle is used to toggle between venting (turned toward the front of the pot) and sealing (turned toward the back of the pot).

Controls

The front of your Instant Pot features a control display with buttons that allow you to manually operate your pot as well as preprogrammed keys for common functions.

When looking at your pot, the first thing you'll likely notice is the LED time display. This display will count down the amount of time your food has been cooking under pressure. When on the Keep Warm setting, the display will count up. This makes it easy to know how much time has lapsed when performing a Natural Pressure Release.

Beneath the time display, you'll see two pressure indicators, which will light up to signify if your pot is programmed to cook under high or low pressure. You'll also see three mode indicators, which you'll use for the Sauté or Slow Cook functions.

At the bottom of the time display, you'll see the +/- keys, which are used to adjust the timer.

Surrounding the LED display are several control buttons as follows:

Pressure Level: Press this key to toggle between high and low pressure.

Keep Warm: If you don't plan to eat your meal right away, the Keep Warm setting will keep your cooked food at a safe temperature for up to 10 hours. You can enable this feature at the beginning of the cooking process or at any time after the process has started.

Delay Start: Use the Delay Start button if you don't want to start the pressure cooking process right away. To use this function, choose your pressure cook settings, and then press the Delay Start button. Use the +/- buttons to set the timer. Pressure will begin to build once the time has expired. This is useful when doing things like soaking dried beans, but keep in mind that it does not keep uncooked meat at a safe temperature.

Cancel: Use this button to stop cooking at any time.

Key Terminology

You're likely to come across some terms that are specific to cooking in an Instant Pot. At first, it may seem like another language, but you'll catch on quickly.

Quick Pressure Release (QPR): Quick Release means letting the pressure out of the pot very quickly, and it is typically used for delicate foods that you don't want to overcook. To perform a Quick Release, switch the valve from the Sealing position to Venting. Stand back—hot steam will immediately begin to shoot through the valve.

Natural Pressure Release (NPR): Natural Release allows the pressure to release slowly. Use this option for starchy recipes and meats and keep in mind that whatever is in the pot will continue to cook during this time. The pot will automatically begin to release pressure naturally when the cooking time has expired, so you don't need to do anything further. The process can take 5 to 30 minutes, depending on how much liquid is inside the pot. You'll know that the pressure has dissipated when the float valve drops. Many recipes will have you perform a Natural Release for a set amount of time, then a Quick Release for the remaining pressure to speed up the process.

Pot in Pot Cooking: This is a cooking method where you put food into a smaller cooking vessel, such as a cake pan or ramekin, and place it on the trivet inside the inner pot. You'll use this technique to make breads, cakes, and casseroles that you don't want to come in contact with additional liquid. You can also use this method to cook two different components of a dish at the same time.

How to Use the Instant Pot

Ready to cook in your Instant Pot for the first time? Here's a step-by-step overview of the process that you'll need to follow.

1. If you want to precook or brown some ingredients, press Sauté. Add your ingredients and cook as desired.

2. Add the remaining ingredients to the pot.

3. Make sure the sealing ring is in its proper position inside the lid.

4. Place the lid on the pot and twist it a quarter turn to the right. A chime will let you know the lid has been properly locked in place.

5. Make sure the steam valve is in the Sealing position. If the valve is set to Venting, the pot will not come to pressure.

6. To set the pressure level manually, press the Pressure Cook button, then select the Pressure Level button to toggle between high and low pressure. Use the +/- buttons to set the timer.

7. Wait for the pot to come to pressure. While the pressure inside the pot starts to build, it won't look like anything is happening. This process can take 5 to 20 minutes, depending on how much liquid is in the pot. When pressure has been reached, the pot will beep and the timer will start to count down.

8. Wait for your food to cook. Once the time has expired, the pot will sound a series of beeps.

9. Release the pressure. Perform a Quick Release or allow the pressure to release naturally, as indicated by your recipe. Carefully unlock the lid by turning it a quarter turn to the left and remove your food.

10. Some recipes may also call for additional ingredients to be added at this point or instruct you to use the Sauté feature again to bring liquids to a boil and help them reduce before serving.

11. Unplug the base unit and replace the inner pot and lid after washing them.

ADJUSTING RECIPES FOR HIGH-ALTITUDE COOKING

Air pressure is lower at high elevations. This lowers the boiling point of water, meaning that the Instant Pot will pressurize (and cook your food) at a lower temperature. To account for this, you can increase the cooking time listed in the upcoming recipes by 5 percent for every 1,000 feet above 2,000 feet elevation you live, rounding to the nearest whole minute.

For example, Denver, Colorado, is a little over 5,200 feet elevation, so if you live there, you'll need to increase your cooking time by 15 percent. That means a recipe like Minestrone Soup (page 52), which typically needs 20 minutes of cooking time, needs to cook for 23 minutes. Flagstaff, Arizona, with an elevation of nearly 7,000 feet, would require 25 minutes.

Adjusting for Different Pot Sizes

Most recipes, including the ones in this book, are written for 6-quart pots, but it's easy to adjust them if your pot is a different size. For a 3-quart pot, simply cut the recipe in half. If you have an 8-quart Instant Pot, check to see if the recipe includes at least 2 cups of liquid; if it does, you're good to go. If the recipe has less liquid than that, you'll need to scale it up; most recipes can be doubled without any issues.

Always keep an eye on the max fill line and remember that the cooking times will stay the same no matter what size pot you use; however, the time it takes for the pot to come to pressure will depend on the amount of food you are cooking.

Stocking Your Clean Eating Kitchen

Stocking your kitchen with healthy foods is one of the most important things you can do to set yourself up for success. Having lots of healthy options within reach means you'll always be able to prepare a nutritious, flavorful meal. A few key kitchen tools and Instant Pot accessories will also maximize the versatility of your pot. Although stocking a healthy kitchen can require an initial outlay of money, it will be well worth it when it comes to convenience in the long term.

Refrigerator and Freezer Staples

Fresh ingredients form the backbone of many recipes in this book. Some of my favorites are outlined in the list that follows, but be sure to adapt them to your own personal tastes and buy produce that you can get excited about. It doesn't matter how much kale you buy; you won't want to eat it if you don't like it.

Fresh leafy greens: Greens such as spinach, chard, and kale can be stirred into soups and stews for added nutritional value or served as a side salad to round out starchier recipes.

Slaw mix: Coleslaw and broccoli slaw mixes are an easy shortcut that allow you to add a variety of vegetables to your pot with no chopping required.

Hard cheeses: Parmesan and aged Cheddar last a long time, and it takes only a little of either to add loads of flavor to your meals.

Fresh or frozen produce: Ingredients such as carrots, zucchini, broccoli, and bell peppers are the starting point for some of my favorite recipes. Fresh produce is best when it's in season; otherwise, frozen always works.

Double concentrated tomato paste: Sold in sealable tubes that store in the refrigerator, using a squeeze of this paste is a great way to add even more depth of flavor to tomato-based recipes than traditional canned tomato paste provides.

Citrus fruits: Lemons and limes will add a great pop of acidity to your recipes and perk up their flavor without adding salt.

Fresh herbs: Cilantro, basil, and other herbs ramp up the flavor of simple recipes. Adding chopped herbs as a garnish to finished recipes also adds an appetizing pop of color and freshness.

Frozen berries: I love having berries on hand to add nutrition to breakfasts and desserts.

Greek yogurt: Whether you purchase it or make your own in the Instant Pot, a scoop of plain yogurt adds richness to soups and casseroles.

Pantry Staples

The recipes in this book lean heavily on a few pantry staples that combine with fresh ingredients for flavorful, nutritious meals. You probably already have a lot of these in your kitchen, but there might be some that you need to purchase. As a general rule, look for packaged items that contain five or fewer whole food ingredients.

Beans and lentils: Using these is a great way to add fiber and protein to your meals.

Canned coconut milk: Coconut milk adds a creamy element to many recipes.

Coconut aminos: Coconut aminos are a minimally processed, gluten-free alternative to soy sauce. If you can't find them, tamari is another option.

Garlic and onions: Almost every savory recipe I make starts with one (or both) of these ingredients. Stock up every time you go to the grocery store.

Brown rice: Brown rice comes out so well when you cook it in the Instant Pot. I use it in many recipes or serve it as a side dish.

Dried spices: Pick one or two international flavor profiles and stock up. Having a variety of spices on hand means you can make everything from Indian curries to spicy chili.

Oats: More than just a breakfast cereal, oats can be ground into flour to make delicious gluten-free baked goods.

Barley: Besides rice, barley is another one of my go-to grains. It has a soft, chewy texture that's great in stews or as a breakfast porridge.

Low-sodium stock: The Instant Pot requires liquid in order to work properly. Using stock instead of water infuses your dishes with even more flavor.

Canned tomatoes: No-salt-added tomatoes are a staple ingredient for soups and stews and can also be used to make Restaurant-Style Salsa (page 117) and Marinara Sauce (page 118). I prefer fire-roasted varieties, which add a subtle smokey element.

Honey and maple syrup: Honey and pure maple syrup are my natural sweeteners of choice.

Whole-grain or gluten-free pasta: Yes, you can make pasta in an Instant Pot! Stock up on whole-grain or gluten-free pasta, depending on your dietary preferences.

Spelt flour: In addition to oat flour, spelt flour is one of my most-used healthy flours. It has a mild flavor that's more akin to white flour than other whole grain flours.

Equipment Essentials

The recipes in this book don't require a lot of equipment beyond the Instant Pot and the trivet that comes along with it, but here are some common utensils and pieces of cookware that will be helpful to have.

7-well egg bite mold: This is my absolute favorite Instant Pot accessory, and it is vital for making egg bites, muffins, and other small treats.

Long-handled tongs: A pair of tongs with a long handle makes it easy to lift items from the bottom of the pot.

Wooden spoon: A wooden spoon is essential for scraping up any browned bits from the bottom of the pot after you use the Sauté function.

6-inch cake pan: A small cake pan is essential for baked goods and some casseroles that might burn if they come into contact with the bottom of the pot. In a pinch, you can fashion a makeshift pan from aluminum foil, but it can get messy.

Steaming basket with handles: Although you can steam items on top of the provided trivet, a steaming basket has smaller holes so food is less likely to fall through. Look for one with long handles to make it easier to lift foods from the pot.

Nonstick insert: Replacing the stainless-steel insert with a nonstick ceramic-coated version can help you avoid the dreaded burn warning from showing up on your display and make cleanup easier.

TROUBLESHOOTING

Once you get the hang of it, using your Instant Pot will be a breeze. But, like any appliance, it isn't completely foolproof. There are several common problems that even seasoned pressure cooker enthusiasts can run into. Keeping the solutions to these common issues in mind will help set you up for success.

Pot won't pressurize. If you don't add enough water or broth, there won't be enough steam produced and the Instant Pot won't pressurize. A good rule of thumb is to add at least 1 cup of liquid to 6-quart models, although some recipes won't need that much because the ingredients will release liquid as they cook. Also, make sure you check that the sealing ring is secured in place. If it isn't, steam can escape from under the lid, which will prevent the pot from pressurizing.

Food comes out soggy. Liquid won't evaporate during the cooking process as it does when you cook on the stove top so using too much will have a stark effect. If your recipe comes out soggy, hit the Sauté button and simmer it for a few minutes, uncovered, until the liquid reduces.

Burn warning. Some ingredients, such as dairy and tomato sauce, have a tendency to stick to the bottom of the pot and trigger a burn warning on the Instant Pot's display. It's important to layer these ingredients on top of everything else. This message can also display if your pot isn't sealed tightly and too much liquid evaporates or if food gets stuck to the bottom. If you see this warning, press Cancel and check to make sure the steam valve and sealing ring are positioned properly. Scrape up any food that's stuck to the bottom of the pot and add more liquid as necessary, then restart the cooking process.

Food is undercooked. Because you can't remove the lid until the pressure has been released, it can be tricky to gauge how long your recipe needs to cook. This is especially true for ingredients such as dried beans and grains from the back of your pantry, as they tend to take longer than their fresh counterparts. If yours need more time, replace the lid and program the pot for another 5 minutes; it will return to pressure very quickly because it's already hot. Alternatively, hit the Sauté button and simmer until done.

Not planning enough time. Remember to factor in time for the pot to come to pressure and release that pressure. All the recipes in this book include a total time estimate that accounts for the time it takes for the pot to pressurize.

The Recipes in This Book

This book contains a collection of my favorite recipes made with wholesome foods all cooked entirely in the Instant Pot. Every recipe was written with ease-of-use in mind and contains 10 ingredients or fewer (not counting oil, salt, pepper, and water).

To accommodate different lifestyles and nutritional needs, I have included a variety of both plant-based and meat-based dishes, as well as labels indicating if they are vegetarian, vegan, gluten-free, nut-free, dairy-free, grain-free. I've also included helpful tips for swapping out ingredients or playing with flavors for added versatility. For those who are short on time, I've included a label for recipes that are especially quick (complete in 30 minutes or less from start to finish).

DF Dairy-Free	**Q** Quick
GF Gluten-Free	**VE** Vegan
GRF Grain-Free	**VG** Vegetarian
NF Nut-Free	

The recipes in this book were all designed to be made in a standard 6-quart Instant Pot and yield four to six servings, which is perfect for a small family or one or two people who love having leftovers. If you're working with a different-size pot, you can scale them up or down (see "How to Use the Instant Pot" on page 12).

I love experimenting with simple, whole food versions of recipes and look for inspiration everywhere I go. To that end, it's important to note that although I'm frequently inspired by the bold flavors of my favorite cultural restaurants, the recipes in this book are made with ingredients that are easily sourced in major grocery stores across the country. If you enjoy the international-inspired cuisine in this book, be sure to check out local restaurants in your neighborhood to experience the authentic versions.

It's my sincere hope that this book makes you fall in love with both clean eating and pressure cooking. The two work so well together, and I know this is just the beginning of many wholesome, delicious, satisfying meals in your future.

Chapter 2

Breakfast

Whole-Grain Blueberry Muffins
PAGE 24

Apple Cinnamon Steel Cut Oats

Steel cut oats are less processed than rolled oats, with a slightly nutty flavor and chewy texture that I love. They take longer to cook than rolled oats on the stove top, but the Instant Pot cuts that cooking time in half and is mostly hands-off, which is great for hectic mornings. I add apples to the pot so they soften like the oatmeal I used to eat when I was a kid. Gala apples are my favorite, but you can use any type.

SERVES 4

PREP TIME: 5 minutes

COOK SETTING: High Pressure for 4 minutes

RELEASE: Natural

TOTAL TIME: 30 minutes

2 cups water

1 cup gluten-free steel cut oats

2 apples, peeled and diced

1 teaspoon ground cinnamon

1 teaspoon vanilla extract

½ teaspoon kosher salt

¼ cup pure maple syrup

1. In the Instant Pot, combine the water, oats, apples, cinnamon, vanilla, and salt. Lock the lid in place.

2. Select Manual or Pressure Cook and set the cooker to High Pressure for 4 minutes.

3. When the cook time is complete, let the pressure release naturally for about 15 minutes, then quick release any remaining pressure.

4. Carefully remove the lid and stir in the maple syrup. Serve warm.

INGREDIENT TIP: Oats are naturally gluten-free, but they frequently become cross-contaminated with wheat in the field or during processing. If gluten is a concern for you or someone you're cooking for, be sure to buy certified gluten-free oats.

Per serving (1 cup): Calories: 264; Fat: 3g; Protein: 5g; Total Carbs: 55g; Fiber: 6g; Sugar: 21g; Sodium: 148mg

Citrusy Buckwheat Porridge

Buckwheat is a gluten-free grain with a mild flavor and a chewy, tapioca-like texture. Think of it as a blank canvas to highlight whatever flavors you mix in. For this citrusy porridge, I like to use a combination of oranges and grapefruit, but you can use just one fruit or add more if you prefer.

SERVES 6

PREP TIME: 5 minutes

COOK SETTING: High Pressure for 6 minutes

RELEASE: Natural

TOTAL TIME: 35 minutes

1 cup buckwheat groats

2 cups canned coconut milk

1 cup water

1 teaspoon kosher salt

½ teaspoon vanilla extract

2 teaspoons honey

1 cup peeled, chopped citrus fruit of choice

1. In the Instant Pot, combine the buckwheat, coconut milk, water, salt, and vanilla. Stir until the buckwheat is submerged and the coconut milk is smooth. Lock the lid in place.

2. Select Manual or Pressure Cook and set the cooker to High Pressure for 6 minutes.

3. When the cook time is complete, let the pressure release naturally for 15 minutes, then quick release any remaining pressure.

4. Carefully remove the lid and stir in the honey and fruit. Serve warm.

INGREDIENT TIP: This porridge can be made with whole grain buckwheat groats or buckwheat hot cereal, which has a smoother texture (think oatmeal compared to cream of wheat).

Per serving (⅙ recipe): Calories: 265; Fat: 17g; Protein: 5g; Total Carbs: 28g; Fiber: 3g; Sugar: 4g; Sodium: 207mg

Whole-Grain Blueberry Muffins

Spelt is an ancient grain that's a primitive relative to modern wheat. It's easily digestible and has more protein than all-purpose flour, with a soft texture that makes it perfect for baked goods (look for it in the baking aisle). It also has a subtle bran flavor. These muffins remind me of the blueberry bran muffins my mom used to bake when I went back to school every September.

MAKES 6 MUFFINS

PREP TIME: 10 minutes

COOK SETTING: High Pressure for 10 minutes

RELEASE: Natural

TOTAL TIME: 40 minutes

Nonstick cooking spray

1 cup spelt flour

1 teaspoon baking powder

¼ teaspoon baking soda

⅛ teaspoon kosher salt

1 egg, beaten

3 tablespoons non-
   dairy milk

2 tablespoons coconut
   oil, melted

2 tablespoons honey

1 teaspoon vanilla extract

½ cup fresh or frozen
   blueberries

1. Grease the outer 6 wells of a 7-well silicone egg bite mold with nonstick cooking spray.

2. In a medium bowl, combine the flour, baking powder, baking soda, and salt.

3. In a small bowl, whisk together the egg, milk, coconut oil, honey, and vanilla. Add the egg mixture to the flour mixture and stir until combined into a thick batter.

4. Divide the batter between the prepared egg bite wells, filling each well about halfway. Gently press the blueberries into the top of each muffin. Place the lid on the mold.

5. Pour 1 cup of water into the Instant Pot and insert the trivet. Place the egg bite mold on top of the trivet.

6. Place the lid on the Instant Pot and lock it in place. Select Manual or Pressure Cook and set the cooker to High Pressure for 10 minutes.

7. When the cook time is complete, let the pressure release naturally for 10 minutes, then quick release any remaining pressure.

8. Carefully remove the lid and lift out the mold. Uncover the muffins and let them cool for 3 to 5 minutes, until the mold is cool to the touch, then pop the muffins out. Serve warm or store at room temperature in an airtight container for up to 3 days.

SUBSTITUTION TIP: For a gluten-free version of these muffins, swap the spelt flour for 1 cup of gluten-free oat flour.

Per serving (1 muffin): Calories: 136; Fat: 6g; Protein: 3g; Total Carbs: 18g; Fiber: 2g; Sugar: 8g; Sodium: 124mg

Pumpkin Pie Oatmeal Bites

The texture of these sweet bites is a cross between pumpkin pie and a muffin: They're firm enough to pick up but soft enough to eat with a spoon. If you don't have an egg bite mold, you can make them in pressure-safe four-ounce canning jars. If you go this route, grab a spoon and eat the oatmeal bites straight from the jars.

MAKES 6 BITES

PREP TIME: 10 minutes

COOK SETTING: High Pressure for 10 minutes

RELEASE: Natural

TOTAL TIME: 35 minutes

Nonstick cooking spray

1 egg, beaten

¾ cup pumpkin puree

3 tablespoons honey

¾ cup gluten-free
   rolled oats

¼ cup spelt flour or white
   whole-wheat flour

1 teaspoon baking powder

1 teaspoon pumpkin
   pie spice

¼ teaspoon kosher salt

INGREDIENT TIP: Make your own pumpkin pie spice mix by combining 2 teaspoons ground cinnamon, 1 teaspoon ground ginger, and ¼ teaspoon each ground cloves and ground nutmeg.

1. Grease the outer 6 wells of a 7-well silicone egg bite mold with nonstick cooking spray.

2. In a medium bowl, whisk the egg, then stir in the pumpkin puree and honey until combined. Mix in the oats, flour, baking powder, pumpkin pie spice, and salt.

3. Divide the batter between the prepared egg wells, filling each well about halfway. Place the lid on the mold or cover it with aluminum foil.

4. Pour 1 cup of water into the Instant Pot and insert the trivet. Place the egg bite mold on top of the trivet. Lock the lid in place.

5. Select Manual or Pressure Cook and set the cooker to High Pressure for 10 minutes.

6. When the cook time is complete, let the pressure release naturally for 10 minutes, then quick release any remaining pressure.

7. Carefully remove the lid and lift out the mold. Uncover the oatmeal bites and let them cool for 4 to 5 minutes before unmolding them. Serve warm or at room temperature.

Per serving (1 oatmeal bite): Calories: 112; Fat: 2g; Protein: 3g; Total Carbs: 22g; Fiber: 3g; Sugar: 10g; Sodium: 67mg

Banana Bread

This banana bread recipe is so soft and pillowy, you'll have a hard time believing it's gluten-free! It's made with oat flour, which has a neutral flavor and gives baked goods a delicate texture without any additional gums or fillers. Look for it in the baking aisle or make your own by blending gluten-free rolled oats until they resemble a fine powder.

SERVES 6

PREP TIME: 10 minutes

COOK SETTING: High Pressure for 55 minutes

RELEASE: Natural

TOTAL TIME: 1 hour 25 minutes

Nonstick cooking spray

1 ripe banana, peeled

1 large egg, beaten

2 tablespoons honey

1 tablespoon coconut oil, melted

½ teaspoon vanilla extract

1 cup gluten-free oat flour

½ teaspoon baking powder

¼ teaspoon kosher salt

FLAVOR BOOST: Try adding ¼ cup chopped nuts, dried fruit, or unsweetened shredded coconut to the batter.

1. Line a 6-inch cake pan with aluminum foil and grease it with nonstick cooking spray.

2. In a large bowl, mash the banana until it's smooth. Whisk in the egg, honey, coconut oil, and vanilla and mix until everything is incorporated. Stir in the flour, baking powder, and salt to form a smooth batter.

3. Pour the batter into the prepared cake pan. Cover the top of the pan with foil.

4. Pour 1 cup of water into the Instant Pot and insert the trivet. Place the cake pan on top of the trivet. Lock the lid in place.

5. Select Manual or Pressure Cook and set the cooker to High Pressure for 55 minutes.

6. When the cook time is complete, let the pressure release naturally for 15 minutes, then quick release any remaining pressure.

7. Carefully remove the lid and lift out the pan. Remove the foil cover and let the banana bread cool for 10 minutes on the trivet. Lift the bread from the pan and cut it into six wedges. Serve warm or at room temperature.

Per serving (1 slice): Calories: 145; Fat: 5g; Protein: 4g; Total Carbs: 23g; Fiber: 2g; Sugar: 9g; Sodium: 68mg

Boiled Eggs

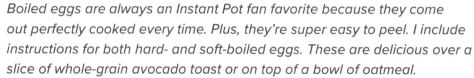

Boiled eggs are always an Instant Pot fan favorite because they come out perfectly cooked every time. Plus, they're super easy to peel. I include instructions for both hard- and soft-boiled eggs. These are delicious over a slice of whole-grain avocado toast or on top of a bowl of oatmeal.

MAKES 6 EGGS

PREP TIME: 5 minutes

COOK SETTING:
High Pressure for
5 minutes (hard-boiled);
Low Pressure for 6 minutes
(soft-boiled)

RELEASE: Natural (hard-boiled); Quick (soft-boiled)

TOTAL TIME: 20 minutes

6 large eggs

1. Pour 1 cup of water into the Instant Pot and insert the trivet. Place the eggs on top of the trivet. Lock the lid in place.

2. Fill a large bowl with ice water and set it aside.

3. **For hard-boiled eggs:** Select Manual or Pressure Cook and set the cooker to High Pressure for 5 minutes. When the cook time is complete, let the pressure release naturally for 5 minutes, then quick release any remaining pressure.

4. **For soft-boiled eggs:** Select Manual or Pressure Cook and set the cooker to Low Pressure for 6 minutes. When the cook time is complete, quick release the pressure.

5. Carefully remove the lid and transfer the eggs to the ice water. Let the eggs sit in the ice water for 5 minutes, then peel and serve.

Per serving (1 egg): Calories: 72; Fat: 5g; Protein: 6g; Total Carbs: 0g; Fiber: 0g; Sugar: 0g; Sodium: 71mg

Ham and Swiss Egg Bites

These individually portioned egg bites are perfect for meal prep. I love making a batch of them and reheating them in the microwave for a superfast breakfast all week long. If you don't have an egg bite mold, you can make these in 4-ounce canning jars. Be sure the jars are labeled "pressure-safe"; other jars are not safe to use in a pressure cooker.

MAKES 12 BITES

PREP TIME: 10 minutes

COOK SETTING: High Pressure for 12 minutes

RELEASE: Natural

TOTAL TIME: 40 minutes

Nonstick cooking spray

8 large eggs, beaten

½ cup milk of choice

½ cup shredded Swiss cheese

½ cup finely diced red bell pepper

¼ cup diced uncured ham

½ teaspoon kosher salt

½ teaspoon freshly ground black pepper

SUBSTITUTION TIP: For a vegetarian version of these egg bites, replace the ham with up to ¼ cup of chopped broccoli or spinach.

1. Grease the outer 6 wells of two 7-well silicone egg bite molds with nonstick cooking spray.

2. In a medium bowl, whisk the eggs and milk until frothy. Stir in the cheese, bell pepper, ham, salt, and black pepper.

3. Divide the egg mixture between the prepared egg bite wells, filling each well about three-quarters full. Cover the molds with their lids or aluminum foil.

4. Pour 1 cup of water into the Instant Pot and insert the trivet. Stack the egg bite molds on top of the trivet. Lock the lid in place.

5. Select Manual or Pressure Cook and set the cooker to High Pressure for 12 minutes.

6. When the cook time is complete, let the pressure release naturally for 10 minutes, then quick release any remaining pressure.

7. Carefully remove the lid and let the eggs cool for a minute or two before releasing them from the molds. Serve warm.

Per serving (2 egg bites): Calories: 152; Fat: 10g; Protein: 13g; Total Carbs: 3g; Fiber: 0g; Sugar: 2g; Sodium: 306mg

Spinach and Feta Crustless Quiche

Cooking quiche in the moist heat of a pressure cooker results in a velvety smooth, creamy custard with the perfect amount of jiggle. Once you've tried it, you'll never want to make a traditional baked quiche again! Using frozen spinach makes this quiche super simple to make. You can break up any large clumps of spinach with your hands, but there's no need to thaw it before adding it to the pan.

SERVES 4

PREP TIME: 5 minutes

COOK SETTING: High Pressure for 30 minutes

RELEASE: Natural

TOTAL TIME: 50 minutes

Nonstick cooking spray
6 large eggs, beaten
¼ cup skim milk
¼ cup crumbled feta
1 shallot, finely chopped
¼ teaspoon kosher salt
¼ teaspoon freshly ground
  black pepper
2 cups frozen
  chopped spinach

1. Grease a 6-inch cake pan with nonstick cooking spray.

2. In a large bowl, whisk together the eggs and milk until frothy. Stir in the feta, shallot, salt, and pepper.

3. Spread the spinach over the bottom of the prepared cake pan, then pour the egg mixture over the spinach. Cover the pan with aluminum foil.

4. Pour 1 cup of water into the Instant Pot and insert the trivet. Place the cake pan on top of the trivet. Lock the lid in place.

5. Select Manual or Pressure Cook and set the cooker to High Pressure for 30 minutes.

6. When the cook time is complete, let the pressure release naturally for 10 minutes, then quick release any remaining pressure.

7. Carefully remove the lid and lift out the cake pan. Cut the quiche into four slices and serve.

VARIATION TIP: Don't like feta? Swap in shredded Swiss or Cheddar cheese.

Per serving (1 slice): Calories: 162; Fat: 10g; Protein: 14g; Total Carbs: 5g; Fiber: 2g; Sugar: 2g; Sodium: 334mg

Sweet Potato Hash

The ingredients in this hash seem simple, but together, they add up to a lot of flavor. A pinch of cayenne pepper balances out the sweetness of the potatoes without adding too much heat to the final dish. If you're sensitive to spicy foods, you can leave it out.

SERVES 4

PREP TIME: 10 minutes

COOK SETTING: Sauté for 10 minutes, then High Pressure for 3 minutes

RELEASE: Quick

TOTAL TIME: 30 minutes

1 tablespoon olive oil

1½ pounds sweet potatoes, peeled and diced

1 yellow onion, chopped

1 red bell pepper, seeded and chopped

2 garlic cloves, minced

1 teaspoon dried oregano

½ teaspoon cayenne pepper

½ teaspoon kosher salt

¼ teaspoon freshly ground black pepper

½ cup Vegetable Broth (page 116) or store-bought low-sodium vegetable broth

4 large eggs

1. Select Sauté on the Instant Pot and pour in the olive oil. When the oil is hot, add the sweet potatoes and cook for 10 minutes, stirring occasionally, until the potatoes begin to brown and soften. Stir in the onion, bell pepper, garlic, oregano, cayenne pepper, salt, and black pepper until well combined. Press Cancel.

2. Stir in the broth, then crack the eggs on top of the potato mixture. Lock the lid in place.

3. Select Manual or Pressure Cook and set the cooker to High Pressure for 3 minutes.

4. When the cook time is complete, quick release the pressure.

5. Carefully remove the lid and serve.

VARIATION TIP: Not a fan of sweet potato? Try this recipe with cubed butternut squash. Shorten the cooking time in step 1 to 5 minutes.

Per serving (¼ recipe): Calories: 271; Fat: 8g; Protein: 10g; Total Carbs: 40g; Fiber: 6g; Sugar: 10g; Sodium: 313mg

Vegetable Tortilla Española

The first time I heard of a Spanish tortilla was when I was traveling. I ordered one at a restaurant and was surprised when, instead of the wrap I was expecting, the server handed me what looked like a frittata. A Spanish tortilla, or tortilla Española, is similar to a hearty frittata that's layered with potatoes and often onions. Here, I swapped out half of the potato for sliced zucchini to vary the flavor and add more nutrition.

SERVES 6

PREP TIME: 5 minutes

COOK SETTING: Sauté for 6 minutes, then High Pressure for 30 minutes

RELEASE: Natural

TOTAL TIME: 1 hour

Nonstick cooking spray

1 tablespoon olive oil

½ cup thinly sliced Yukon Gold potato

½ cup thinly sliced zucchini

½ cup thinly sliced yellow onion

6 large eggs, beaten

¼ teaspoon kosher salt

¼ teaspoon freshly ground black pepper

1. Grease a 6-inch cake pan with nonstick cooking spray.

2. Select Sauté on the Instant Pot and pour in the olive oil. When the oil is hot, add the potato, zucchini, and onion. Cook, stirring occasionally, for about 6 minutes, until the onions begin to brown and the potatoes crisp. Press Cancel. Transfer the cooked vegetables to the prepared cake pan.

3. In a large bowl, whisk together the eggs, salt, and pepper. Pour the egg mixture over the vegetables. Cover the top of the cake pan with aluminum foil.

4. Pour 1 cup of water into the Instant Pot and insert the trivet. Place the cake pan on top of the trivet. Lock the lid in place.

5. Select Manual or Pressure Cook and set the cooker to High Pressure for 30 minutes.

6. When the cook time is complete, let the pressure release naturally for 10 minutes, then quick release any remaining pressure.

7. Carefully remove the lid and lift out the cake pan. Uncover the tortilla and let it cool for 10 minutes on the trivet, then cut it into six wedges. Serve warm.

INGREDIENT TIP: If you have a mandoline, this is a great time to pull it out. Slicing the potatoes paper-thin will help them crisp up.

Per serving (1 slice): Calories: 107; Fat: 7g; Protein: 7g; Total Carbs: 4g; Fiber: 1g; Sugar: 1g; Sodium: 125mg

Chapter 3

Snacks and Sides

Potato and Snap Pea Salad
PAGE 43

35

Unsweetened Applesauce

Growing up in Upstate New York, it never truly felt like fall until we spent a day at the apple orchard. We'd always come home and make a giant pot of applesauce. My version is thick and chunky with a hint of cinnamon that makes it taste like pie filling. It's delicious as a snack, but you can also use it to replace oil in baked goods or add natural sweetness to homemade barbecue sauce.

SERVES 6

PREP TIME: 5 minutes

COOK SETTING: High Pressure for 8 minutes

RELEASE: Natural

TOTAL TIME: 30 minutes

6 apples (about 1½ pounds)

¼ cup water

¼ teaspoon ground cinnamon

1. Peel and core the apples. Cut each apple into roughly eight large chunks.

2. In the Instant Pot, combine the apples, water, and cinnamon. Lock the lid in place.

3. Select Manual or Pressure Cook and set the cooker to High Pressure for 8 minutes.

4. When the cook time is complete, let the pressure release naturally for 10 minutes, then quick release any remaining pressure.

5. Carefully remove the lid and use a potato masher or heavy wooden spoon to gently mash the apples into applesauce.

6. Serve warm or refrigerate in an airtight container for up to 10 days.

INGREDIENT TIP: The type of apples you use will affect the final flavor and texture of your applesauce. I love using Gala apples, which have a naturally sweet flavor. Other great options include Golden Delicious, Fuji, and Cortland apples.

Per serving (⅓ cup): Calories: 95; Fat: 0g; Protein: 0g; Total Carbs: 25g; Fiber: 4g; Sugar: 19g; Sodium: 2mg

Classic Hummus

Once you've made your own hummus from dried chickpeas, you'll never want to go back to store-bought versions again. Even the most basic recipe is so flavorful. Adding baking powder to the cooking liquid helps the skins of the chickpeas dissolve, resulting in an extra-creamy dip. If you don't have an immersion blender, you can use a potato masher in the final step, but your hummus won't be as silky smooth. Another option is to blend the mixture in a food processor.

MAKES 1½ CUPS

PREP TIME: 5 minutes

COOK SETTING: High Pressure for 1 hour

RELEASE: Natural

TOTAL TIME: 1 hour 25 minutes

¾ cup dried chickpeas

1½ cups water

4 garlic cloves

½ teaspoon baking soda

2 tablespoons tahini

1 tablespoon freshly squeezed lemon juice

¼ teaspoon kosher salt

¼ teaspoon ground cumin (optional)

1. In the Instant Pot, combine the chickpeas, water, garlic, and baking soda. Lock the lid in place.

2. Select Manual or Pressure Cook and set the cooker to High Pressure for 1 hour.

3. When the cook time is complete, let the pressure release naturally for 15 minutes, then quick release any remaining pressure.

4. Carefully remove the lid and stir in the tahini and lemon juice. Use an immersion blender to puree the hummus into a smooth paste. Season with salt and cumin (if using). Serve warm or chilled.

5. Store leftovers in an airtight container in the refrigerator for up to a week.

FLAVOR BOOST: Add ½ cup of roasted red peppers to the cooked chickpeas before blending.

Per serving (¼ cup): Calories: 128; Fat: 4g; Protein: 6g; Total Carbs: 18g; Fiber: 4g; Sugar: 3g; Sodium: 169mg

Refried Beans

Refried beans are one of my favorite side dishes. You'll love how silky they come out when you start with dried pinto beans. I like to leave some texture to the beans when mashing them, but for more of a canned style, you can mash until they're completely smooth. If you like your refried beans thicker, select Sauté after pressure cooking and cook, uncovered, for 5 to 10 minutes before serving.

SERVES 6

PREP TIME: 5 minutes

COOK SETTING: High Pressure for 1 hour

RELEASE: Natural

TOTAL TIME: 1 hour 30 minutes

6 cups Chicken Stock (page 115) or store-bought chicken stock

3 cups dried pinto beans

1 yellow onion, diced

1 tablespoon apple cider vinegar

2 teaspoons ground cumin

½ teaspoon kosher salt

1. In the Instant Pot, combine the stock, beans, onion, vinegar, cumin, and salt. Lock the lid in place.

2. Select Manual or Pressure Cook and set the cooker to High Pressure for 1 hour.

3. When the cook time is complete, let the pressure release naturally for 15 minutes, then quick release any remaining pressure.

4. Carefully remove the lid. Reserve ½ cup of the bean cooking liquid, then drain the beans. Return the beans to the pot and use an immersion blender or potato masher to blend them to your desired consistency. If the beans are too thick, stir in some of the reserved liquid to thin them out. Serve.

FLAVOR BOOST: Try adding a small can of mild green chiles along with the rest of the ingredients in step 1 for additional flavor.

Per serving (½ cup): Calories: 360; Fat: 1g; Protein: 23g; Total Carbs: 63g; Fiber: 15g; Sugar: 3g; Sodium: 111mg

Classic Black Beans

My Basic Beans (page 114) are great to use in recipes instead of canned beans. But if you're looking for a flavorful side dish that stands on its own, try these classic black beans. They're savory and just a little bit spicy. I love combining them with rice and a vegetable for an easy dinner or topping them with salsa and a fried egg for breakfast.

SERVES 4

PREP TIME: 5 minutes

COOK SETTING: Sauté for 5 minutes, then High Pressure for 40 minutes

RELEASE: Natural

TOTAL TIME: 1 hour 15 minutes

2 tablespoons olive oil

1 yellow onion, diced

1 green bell pepper, seeded and diced

1 jalapeño pepper, seeded and minced

2 garlic cloves, minced

1 teaspoon dried oregano

1 teaspoon ground cumin

1 cup dried black beans

1 tablespoon apple cider vinegar

½ teaspoon kosher salt

1½ cups water

1. Select Sauté on the Instant Pot and pour in the oil. When the oil is hot, add the onion, bell pepper, jalapeño, and garlic. Cook, stirring frequently, for 3 to 5 minutes, until softened. Press Cancel.

2. Stir in the oregano and cumin, then add the beans, vinegar, salt, and water. Lock the lid in place.

3. Select Manual or Pressure Cook and set the cooker to High Pressure for 40 minutes.

4. When the cook time is complete, let the pressure release naturally for 15 minutes, then quick release any remaining pressure.

5. Carefully remove the lid and serve.

INGREDIENT TIP: Planning ahead? If you soak the beans overnight, you can shorten the cooking time in step 3 to 10 minutes.

Per serving (¾ cup): Calories: 249; Fat: 8g; Protein: 11g; Total Carbs: 35g; Fiber: 8g; Sugar: 3g; Sodium: 151mg

Cilantro-Lime Brown Rice

I have terrible luck cooking rice on my stove top. It always boils over or sticks to the bottom of the pot. In the Instant Pot, it comes out perfect every time, with soft, tender grains. Be sure to rinse the rice before adding it to the pot. This will wash away excess starch that can make it come out thick and clumpy.

SERVES 4

PREP TIME: 5 minutes

COOK SETTING: High Pressure for 15 minutes

RELEASE: Natural

TOTAL TIME: 45 minutes

1 cup long-grain brown rice, rinsed

1¼ cups water

Zest and juice of 1 lime

¼ cup freshly chopped cilantro

1 teaspoon kosher salt

1. In the Instant Pot, combine the rice and water. Stir well. Lock the lid in place.

2. Select Manual or Pressure Cook and set the cooker to High Pressure for 15 minutes.

3. When the cook time is complete, let the pressure release naturally for 20 minutes, then quick release any remaining pressure.

4. Carefully remove the lid and stir in the lime zest, lime juice, cilantro, and salt before serving.

FLAVOR BOOST: Use Chicken Stock (page 115) or Vegetable Broth (page 116) in place of the water.

Per serving (½ cup): Calories: 174; Fat: 1g; Protein: 4g; Total Carbs: 37g; Fiber: 2g; Sugar: 0g; Sodium: 295mg

Coconut Rice

Cooking rice in coconut milk results in a creamy side dish that's packed with flavor. It's the perfect accompaniment to spicy Thai- or Caribbean-inspired dishes. Traditionally, this recipe is made with jasmine rice, but I love the toasty flavor and added nutritional value that long-grain brown rice provides.

SERVES 6

PREP TIME: 5 minutes

COOK SETTING: Sauté for 3 minutes, then High Pressure for 15 minutes

RELEASE: Natural

TOTAL TIME: 40 minutes

2 tablespoons unsweet-
    ened shredded coconut

1½ cups long-grain brown
    rice, rinsed

1 (14-ounce) can light
    coconut milk

½ cup water

¼ teaspoon kosher salt

1. Select Sauté on the Instant Pot and pour in the shredded coconut. Cook, stirring frequently, for 2 to 3 minutes or until toasted and golden brown. Press Cancel. Transfer the toasted coconut to a small dish and set aside.

2. In the Instant Pot, combine the rice, coconut milk, water, and salt. Stir well to combine. Lock the lid in place.

3. Select Manual or Pressure Cook and set the cooker to High Pressure for 15 minutes.

4. When the cook time is complete, let the pressure release naturally for 10 minutes, then quick release any remaining pressure.

5. Carefully remove the lid and stir in the toasted coconut before serving.

FLAVOR BOOST: For extra flavor and crunch, sauté 1 thinly sliced shallot in 1 tablespoon of olive oil until it's golden brown and crisp. Dry the shallot on a paper towel and add it with the toasted coconut in step 5.

Per serving (¾ cup): Calories: 307; Fat: 16g; Protein: 5g; Total Carbs: 38g; Fiber: 2g; Sugar: 1g; Sodium: 64mg

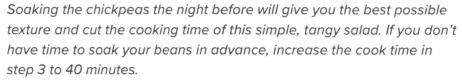

Warm Chickpea Salad

Soaking the chickpeas the night before will give you the best possible texture and cut the cooking time of this simple, tangy salad. If you don't have time to soak your beans in advance, increase the cook time in step 3 to 40 minutes.

SERVES 4

PREP TIME: 5 minutes, plus overnight to soak

COOK SETTING: Sauté for 5 minutes, then High Pressure for 15 minutes

RELEASE: Natural

TOTAL TIME: 40 minutes, plus overnight to soak

2 tablespoons olive oil, plus ¼ cup

1 red onion, diced

1 red bell pepper, seeded and diced

1 zucchini, diced

1 cup dried chickpeas, soaked overnight (see headnote)

3 cups water

1 cup baby spinach

3 tablespoons freshly squeezed lemon juice

¼ teaspoon kosher salt

¼ teaspoon freshly ground black pepper

¼ cup crumbled feta cheese

1 teaspoon dried oregano

1. Select Sauté on the Instant Pot and pour in 2 tablespoons of olive oil. When the oil is hot, add the onion, bell pepper, and zucchini. Cook, stirring frequently, for 4 to 5 minutes, or until softened. Press Cancel.

2. Add the chickpeas and water. Lock the lid in place.

3. Select Manual or Pressure Cook and set the cooker to High Pressure for 15 minutes.

4. When the cook time is complete, let the pressure release naturally for 10 minutes, then quick release any remaining pressure.

5. Carefully remove the lid and stir in the remaining ¼ cup of olive oil, the spinach, lemon juice, salt, and black pepper. Top with the feta and oregano and serve.

SUBSTITUTION TIP: For a plant-based version of this salad, omit the feta and increase the salt by ¼ teaspoon.

Per serving (¼ recipe): Calories: 426; Fat: 26g; Protein: 13g; Total Carbs: 39g; Fiber: 8g; Sugar: 10g; Sodium: 188mg

Potato and Snap Pea Salad

This potato salad quickly became one of my favorite side dishes after I received something similar in a meal box kit a few years ago. It's a vinegar-based salad, similar to German potato salad, but with snap peas instead of bacon. The peas add a satisfying crunch and peppery bite that I love. Steaming the potatoes in the Instant Pot ensures they come out tender and creamy and shaves time off the cooking process.

SERVES 6

PREP TIME: 10 minutes

COOK SETTING: High Pressure for 4 minutes

RELEASE: Quick

TOTAL TIME: 25 minutes

1½ pounds (4 or 5) yellow potatoes

1 shallot, finely chopped

¼ cup apple cider vinegar

¼ cup olive oil

1 teaspoon Dijon mustard

½ teaspoon kosher salt

4 ounces sugar snap peas, halved lengthwise

1. Cut each potato into 12 pieces by cutting it in half lengthwise, cutting each half lengthwise again, then cutting each of those pieces crosswise into thirds.

2. In a large bowl, whisk together the shallot, vinegar, oil, mustard, and salt. Set the dressing aside.

3. Pour 2 cups of water into the Instant Pot and insert the trivet or a steamer basket. Add the potatoes and lock the lid in place.

4. Select Manual or Pressure Cook and set the cooker to High Pressure for 4 minutes.

5. When the cook time is complete, quick release the pressure.

6. Carefully remove the lid and transfer the cooked potatoes to the bowl of dressing. Stir in the peas. Serve this salad warm or chilled.

VARIATION TIP: If you can't find snap peas, try using fresh green beans in this recipe.

Per serving (⅙ recipe): Calories: 179; Fat: 9g; Protein: 6g; Total Carbs: 22g; Fiber: 3g; Sugar: 2g; Sodium: 115mg

Collard Greens

Collard greens are often made with a ham hock or smoked turkey to give them extra flavor, but I use a few slices of sugar-free bacon instead. Bacon gives you that same meaty texture and smoky flavor, but it's easier to find and more affordable. Check the label and be sure to choose a brand with a clean ingredient list, meaning just pork, water, vinegar, spices, and either celery powder or rosemary extract. This recipe is unique in that you don't need to add steaming liquid to the Instant Pot; the greens will release enough on their own as they cook.

SERVES 6

PREP TIME: 5 minutes

COOK SETTING: Sauté for 6 minutes, then High Pressure for 12 minutes

RELEASE: Quick

TOTAL TIME: 30 minutes

---

6 no-sugar-added uncured bacon slices, diced

1 yellow onion, diced

16 ounces frozen chopped collard greens

1 tablespoon apple cider vinegar

¼ teaspoon kosher salt

¼ teaspoon garlic powder

1. Select Sauté on the Instant Pot and add the bacon. Cook for 3 minutes, stirring frequently, until the fat renders. Stir in the onion and cook for 3 minutes, stirring frequently, until soft. Press Cancel.

2. Stir in the collard greens, vinegar, salt, and garlic powder. Use your spoon to scrape up anything that's stuck to the bottom of the pot. Lock the lid in place.

3. Select Manual or Pressure Cook and set the cooker to High Pressure for 12 minutes.

4. When the cook time is complete, quick release the pressure.

5. Carefully remove the lid, stir, and serve.

FLAVOR BOOST: For an extra kick, stir in 1 teaspoon of red pepper flakes along with the other ingredients in step 2.

Per serving (½ cup): Calories: 139; Fat: 11g; Protein: 6g; Total Carbs: 7g; Fiber: 3g; Sugar: 1g; Sodium: 159mg

Garlic Brussels Sprouts

These Brussels sprouts come out of the Instant Pot perfectly tender-crisp and infused with bold, garlicky flavor. I like to sauté my sprouts in olive oil for a few minutes to give them some color. If your sprouts are especially large (the size of a golf ball or bigger) or if you like them very tender, you may need to increase the cook time in step 3 to 3 minutes.

SERVES 6

PREP TIME: 5 minutes

COOK SETTING: Sauté for 4 minutes, then High Pressure for 2 minutes

RELEASE: Quick

TOTAL TIME: 15 minutes

1 tablespoon olive oil

1 pound Brussels sprouts, bottoms trimmed

½ cup Vegetable Broth (page 116) or store-bought low-sodium vegetable broth

5 garlic cloves, minced

¼ teaspoon kosher salt

¼ teaspoon freshly ground black pepper

1. Select Sauté on the Instant Pot and pour in the oil. When the oil is hot, add the Brussels sprouts. Cook undisturbed for 3 to 4 minutes, until lightly browned. Press Cancel.

2. Add the broth and garlic. Lock the lid in place.

3. Select Manual or Pressure Cook and set the cooker to High Pressure for 2 minutes.

4. When the cook time is complete, quick release the pressure.

5. Carefully remove the lid and season with the salt and pepper before serving.

Per serving (⅙ recipe): Calories: 56; Fat: 2g; Protein: 3g; Total Carbs: 8g; Fiber: 3g; Sugar: 2g; Sodium: 71mg

Autumn Acorn Squash

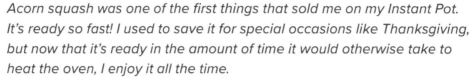

Acorn squash was one of the first things that sold me on my Instant Pot. It's ready so fast! I used to save it for special occasions like Thanksgiving, but now that it's ready in the amount of time it would otherwise take to heat the oven, I enjoy it all the time.

SERVES 4

PREP TIME: 5 minutes

COOK SETTING: High Pressure for 5 minutes

RELEASE: Natural

TOTAL TIME: 20 minutes

2 acorn squash

4 teaspoons coconut oil

4 teaspoons pure
   maple syrup

¼ teaspoon ground
   cinnamon

¼ teaspoon kosher salt

1. Cut the squash in half through the root, then scoop out and discard the seeds. Divide the coconut oil, maple syrup, cinnamon, and salt evenly between the centers of each squash half.

2. Pour 1 cup of water into the Instant Pot and insert the trivet. Stack the squash, cut-side up, on top of the trivet. Lock the lid in place.

3. Select Manual or Pressure Cook and set the cooker to High Pressure for 5 minutes.

4. When the cook time is complete, let the pressure release naturally for 5 minutes, then quick release any remaining pressure.

5. Carefully remove the lid and serve.

SUBSTITUTION TIP: For a side dish that's more on the savory side, swap the cinnamon for chili powder.

Per serving (½ squash): Calories: 142; Fat: 5g; Protein: 2g; Total Carbs: 27g; Fiber: 3g; Sugar: 4g; Sodium: 85mg

Cauliflower Mashed Potatoes

Cauliflower has been the darling of the clean eating world over the last few years, standing in for everything from chicken wings to pizza crust. One of my personal favorite ways to use this versatile vegetable is to add it to mashed potatoes. It gives the potatoes a nutritional boost without an overpowering cauliflower flavor.

SERVES 6

PREP TIME: 10 minutes

COOK SETTING: High Pressure for 8 minutes

RELEASE: Quick

TOTAL TIME: 25 minutes

1 pound potatoes, peeled and cubed

2 cups fresh or frozen cauliflower florets

4 garlic cloves

¼ cup unsweetened nondairy milk, such as almond or coconut

¼ teaspoon kosher salt

½ teaspoon freshly ground black pepper

1. Pour 2 cups of water into the Instant Pot and insert the trivet or a steamer basket. Add the potatoes, cauliflower, and garlic. Lock the lid in place.

2. Select Manual or Pressure Cook and set the cooker to High Pressure for 8 minutes.

3. When the cook time is complete, quick release the pressure.

4. Carefully remove the lid and drain the water. Return the vegetables to the pot and add the milk, salt, and pepper. Use a potato masher to mash the potatoes and cauliflower to your desired consistency, and then serve.

INGREDIENT TIP: For the creamiest mash, choose waxy potatoes like Yukon Gold or red potatoes for this recipe. Starchier potatoes such as russets can have a grainy texture.

Per serving (⅔ cup): Calories: 75; Fat: 0g; Protein: 3g; Total Carbs: 16g; Fiber: 3g; Sugar: 2g; Sodium: 71mg

Smoky Sweet Potatoes

These sweet potatoes are coated with a sweet and smoky glaze that's seriously flavorful. Using the Instant Pot to steam the potatoes before sautéing them with the glaze means they'll be ready to eat in about 15 minutes. They're fantastic as a quick side dish or as a fun topping for a grain bowl. Try them with Cilantro-Lime Brown Rice (page 40) and Classic Black Beans (page 39) for an easy and nourishing meal.

SERVES 4

PREP TIME: 5 minutes

COOK SETTING: High Pressure for 4 minutes, then Sauté for 3 minutes

RELEASE: Quick

TOTAL TIME: 15 minutes

1 pound sweet potatoes (about 2 medium potatoes), cut into ½-inch rounds

2 teaspoons coconut oil

1 teaspoon honey

1 teaspoon chili powder

¼ teaspoon smoked paprika

¼ teaspoon kosher salt

1. Pour ½ cup of water into the Instant Pot, then add the potato slices (no need to use a trivet). Lock the lid in place.

2. Select Manual or Pressure Cook and set the cooker to High Pressure for 4 minutes.

3. When the cook time is complete, quick release the pressure. Press Cancel.

4. Carefully remove the lid and stir in the coconut oil, honey, chili powder, paprika, and salt. Select Sauté and cook for 2 to 3 minutes, stirring occasionally, until the potatoes are coated with a thick glaze. Serve.

INGREDIENT TIP: Keep the skins on the potatoes for this recipe. They'll soften as the potatoes cook and are a valuable source of fiber.

Per serving (¼ recipe): Calories: 125; Fat: 2g; Protein: 2g; Total Carbs: 25g; Fiber: 4g; Sugar: 6g; Sodium: 159mg

Chapter 4

Vegan and Vegetarian

Minestrone Soup
PAGE 52

Minestrone Soup

The Instant Pot is great for making soup, such as this minestrone. Cooking it under pressure gives it that simmered-all-day flavor in just over 30 minutes. The ingredients may seem simple, but they meld together to give the soup a wonderful depth of flavor. I love serving this with a slice of whole-grain bread to soak up every last bit of delicious broth.

SERVES 4

PREP TIME: 5 minutes

COOK SETTING: Sauté for 5 minutes, then High Pressure for 20 minutes

RELEASE: Quick

TOTAL TIME: 35 minutes

---

1 tablespoon olive oil

1 yellow onion, diced

5 garlic cloves, minced

4 cups Vegetable Broth (page 116) or store-bought low-sodium vegetable broth

1 (15-ounce) can cannellini beans, drained and rinsed

1 (14.5-ounce) can fire-roasted diced tomatoes

2 celery stalks, sliced

1 zucchini, chopped

2 teaspoons Italian seasoning

1 teaspoon kosher salt

¼ cup shredded Parmesan cheese

1. Select Sauté on the Instant Pot and pour in the olive oil. When the oil is hot, add the onion and garlic. Cook for 3 to 5 minutes, stirring frequently, until the onions soften. Press Cancel.

2. Add the broth, beans, tomatoes with their juices, celery, zucchini, Italian seasoning, and salt. Lock the lid in place.

3. Select Manual or Pressure Cook and set the cooker to High Pressure for 20 minutes.

4. When the cook time is complete, quick release the pressure.

5. Carefully remove the lid and stir in the Parmesan before serving.

VARIATION TIP: Making this soup is a great way to use up any vegetables that might be hanging out in your refrigerator. Add up to 1 cup of diced hearty vegetables, such as squash or potatoes, in step 2, or stir in 2 cups of leafy greens, such as spinach or kale, in step 5 just before serving.

Per serving (about 2 cups): Calories: 225; Fat: 7g; Protein: 11g; Total Carbs: 32g; Fiber: 3g; Sugar: 5g; Sodium: 523mg

Red Lentil and Swiss Chard Soup

This is one of my absolute favorite soup recipes. It's rich and nourishing, and it feels as though you're giving yourself a giant hug. Unlike brown lentils, which have a starchy texture and hold their shape, red lentils break down as they cook to give this soup an irresistible richness. They're also a great source of fiber.

SERVES 4

PREP TIME: 5 minutes

COOK SETTING: Sauté for 4 minutes, then High Pressure for 10 minutes

RELEASE: Quick

TOTAL TIME: 25 minutes

1 teaspoon olive oil

1 yellow onion, diced

2 carrots, peeled and cut into ½-inch slices

1 bunch Swiss chard, stems and leaves separated, chopped

4 cups Vegetable Broth (page 116) or store-bought low-sodium vegetable broth

1 (14.5-ounce) can no-sodium-added diced tomatoes

1 cup dried red lentils

1 teaspoon ground cumin

½ teaspoon ground turmeric

¾ teaspoon kosher salt

1. Select Sauté on the Instant Pot and pour in the olive oil. When the oil is hot, add the onion, carrots, and chard stems. Sauté for 3 to 4 minutes, until softened. Press Cancel.

2. Stir in the broth, tomatoes with their juices, lentils, cumin, and turmeric. Lock the lid in place.

3. Select Manual or Pressure Cook and set the cooker to High Pressure for 10 minutes.

4. When the cook time is complete, quick release the pressure.

5. Carefully remove the lid. Stir in the chard leaves and salt. Let sit for 3 to 4 minutes, or until the chard wilts, and serve.

INGREDIENT TIP: Always check dried lentils for small stones before adding them to the Instant Pot. To do this, give them a quick rinse in a colander and sift through them with your fingers. You won't find stones very often, but they do show up in dried lentil packages sometimes, and it's worth taking the extra minute to avoid finding one on your spoon.

Per serving (about 2 cups): Calories: 232; Fat: 3g; Protein: 14g; Total Carbs: 41g; Fiber: 9g; Sugar: 6g; Sodium: 317mg

Chickpea Stew with Fennel and Oregano

Stews are typically thought of as winter food, but this Greek-inspired chickpea stew has a light, lemony broth that's perfect for warmer weather. Be sure to use fresh oregano for this recipe. It has a brighter, more intense flavor and a softer texture than dried oregano.

SERVES 4

PREP TIME: 10 minutes

COOK SETTING: High Pressure for 10 minutes

RELEASE: Quick

TOTAL TIME: 30 minutes

5 cups Vegetable Broth (page 116), or store-bought low-sodium vegetable broth

2 (29-ounce) cans chickpeas, drained and rinsed

1 fennel bulb, thinly sliced

1 yellow onion, diced

5 garlic cloves, minced

2 tablespoons whole fresh oregano leaves

½ teaspoon kosher salt

Juice of 1 lemon

½ cup crumbled full-fat feta cheese

1. In the Instant Pot, combine the broth, chickpeas, fennel, onion, garlic, oregano, and salt. Lock the lid in place.

2. Select Manual or Pressure Cook and set the cooker to High Pressure for 10 minutes.

3. When the cook time is complete, quick release the pressure.

4. Carefully remove the lid and stir in the lemon juice. Top each portion with feta before serving.

Per serving (¼ recipe): Calories: 290; Fat: 7g; Protein: 15g; Total Carbs: 44g; Fiber: 12g; Sugar: 11g; Sodium: 358mg

Sweet Potato and Black Bean Chili

I love using sweet potatoes in vegetarian chili. Their natural sweetness contrasts so well with the smoky, spicy flavor of chili powder. Using salsa instead of adding vegetables and tomatoes individually is one of my favorite kitchen shortcuts because it shortens prep time. Cutting the potatoes into ½-inch pieces gives the chili a more consistent texture than leaving them in larger cubes.

SERVES 4

PREP TIME: 5 minutes

COOK SETTING: High Pressure for 5 minutes

RELEASE: Quick

TOTAL TIME: 25 minutes

2 cups Restaurant-Style Salsa (page 117) or store-bought salsa

¼ cup water

2 large sweet potatoes, peeled and cut into ½-inch cubes

2 (15.5-ounce) cans low-sodium black beans, drained and rinsed

2 tablespoons chili powder

1 tablespoon ground cumin

¼ teaspoon kosher salt

¼ teaspoon freshly ground black pepper

¼ teaspoon cayenne pepper (optional)

1. In the Instant Pot, combine the salsa, water, sweet potatoes, beans, chili powder, cumin, salt, black pepper, and cayenne pepper (if using). Lock the lid in place.

2. Select Manual or Pressure Cook and set the cooker to High Pressure for 5 minutes.

3. When the cook time is complete, quick release the pressure.

4. Carefully remove the lid and serve.

FLAVOR BOOST: Sprinkle the chili with pepitas (roasted pumpkin seeds) before serving for extra texture and flavor.

Per serving (¼ recipe): Calories: 281; Fat: 2g; Protein: 15g; Total Carbs: 55g; Fiber: 17g; Sugar: 8g; Sodium: 245mg

Millet Burrito Bowls

Millet is commonly used as a grain, but it's actually harvested from grasses that grow in Asia and Africa. It's naturally gluten-free and has a small, crumbly texture and mild flavor. Look for it at your favorite natural foods store or in the natural section of some larger grocery stores.

SERVES 4

PREP TIME: 5 minutes

COOK SETTING: Sauté for 4 minutes, then High Pressure for 9 minutes

RELEASE: Natural

TOTAL TIME: 30 minutes

---

1 tablespoon olive oil

1 yellow onion, finely diced

1 red bell pepper, seeded and sliced

1 (15.5-ounce) can low-sodium black beans, drained and rinsed

2 cups frozen corn

1 cup millet, rinsed well and drained

1 cup Restaurant-Style Salsa (page 117) or store-bought salsa

¾ cup Vegetable Broth (page 116) or store-bought low-sodium vegetable broth

½ teaspoon kosher salt

¼ cup fresh cilantro, chopped

1. Select Sauté on the Instant Pot and pour in the olive oil. When the oil is hot, add the onion and bell pepper. Cook for 3 to 4 minutes, stirring occasionally, until softened. Press Cancel.

2. Add the beans, corn, millet, salsa, broth, and salt. Stir to combine. Lock the lid in place.

3. Select Manual or Pressure Cook and set the cooker to High Pressure for 9 minutes.

4. When the cook time is complete, let the pressure release naturally for 10 minutes, then quick release any remaining pressure.

5. Carefully remove the lid and stir. Top with the cilantro and serve.

FLAVOR BOOST: These burrito bowls are delicious as is, but you can also serve them with your favorite burrito toppings. I like to add shredded lettuce, sour cream, and hot sauce.

Per serving (¼ recipe): Calories: 426; Fat: 7g; Protein: 15g; Total Carbs: 76g; Fiber: 13g; Sugar: 6g; Sodium: 383mg

Butternut Squash Risotto

Making risotto on the stove top can be tedious, requiring constant stirring for almost an hour. Thankfully, risotto made in the Instant Pot is just as creamy and delicious as traditional versions, but it takes much less effort to make. I use short-grain brown rice for this recipe, which has a slightly nutty flavor and more healthy fiber than white rice.

SERVES 4

PREP TIME: 10 minutes

COOK SETTING: Sauté for 3 minutes, then High Pressure for 15 minutes

RELEASE: Natural

TOTAL TIME: 45 minutes

¼ cup olive oil

1 yellow onion, finely diced

2 garlic cloves, minced

½ ounce (about 10) whole fresh sage leaves

1½ cups short-grain brown rice

4 cups Vegetable Broth (page 116) or store-bought low-sodium vegetable broth

1 small butternut squash, peeled and diced (about 2½ cups)

½ teaspoon kosher salt

¼ teaspoon freshly ground black pepper

3 cups fresh arugula

1. Select Sauté on the Instant Pot and pour in the olive oil. When the oil is hot, add the onion, garlic, and sage. Cook for 3 minutes, stirring frequently, until softened. Press Cancel.

2. Stir in the rice, then add the broth, squash, salt, and pepper. Lock the lid in place.

3. Select Manual or Pressure Cook and set the cooker to High Pressure for 15 minutes.

4. When the cook time is complete, let the pressure release naturally for 10 minutes, then quick release any remaining pressure.

5. Carefully remove the lid and stir in the arugula before serving.

VARIATION TIP: Give mushroom risotto a try: Sauté 4 cups of sliced mixed mushrooms along with the aromatics in step 1. Transfer them to a small dish and set aside. Continue with the recipe as written, omitting the squash, and return the cooked mushrooms to the pot in step 5.

Per serving (¼ recipe): Calories: 434; Fat: 16g; Protein: 7g; Total Carbs: 68g; Fiber: 5g; Sugar: 4g; Sodium: 157mg

Garlicky Lemon-Parmesan Spaghetti Squash

Spaghetti squash is one of the coolest vegetables. This hard-skinned yellow squash breaks down into long, spaghetti-like strands once cooked. It's often served as a healthier alternative to pasta.

SERVES 4

PREP TIME: 10 minutes

COOK SETTING: High Pressure for 10 minutes, then Sauté for 3 minutes

RELEASE: Quick

TOTAL TIME: 30 minutes

2 small (2½- to 3-pound) spaghetti squash

¼ cup olive oil

6 garlic cloves, sliced

Zest and juice of 1 lemon

½ cup shredded Parmesan cheese

¼ cup fresh parsley, chopped

½ teaspoon kosher salt

½ teaspoon freshly ground black pepper

INGREDIENT TIP: For the longest strands of "spaghetti," cut the squash crosswise into rings rather than from end to end.

1. Cut the spaghetti squash in half crosswise and discard the seeds.

2. Pour 1 cup of water into the Instant Pot and insert the trivet. Place the squash on top of the trivet, stacking the halves to fit if necessary, and lock the lid in place.

3. Select Manual or Pressure Cook and set the cooker to High Pressure for 10 minutes. When the cook time is complete, quick release the pressure.

4. Carefully remove the lid. Remove the squash and discard any remaining water. Let the squash rest for about 5 minutes. When it is cool enough to handle, use a fork to scrape the flesh into spaghetti-like strands.

5. Return the inner pot to the base of the Instant Pot. Select Sauté and pour in the olive oil. When the oil is hot, add the garlic and lemon zest. Cook for 2 to 3 minutes, stirring frequently, until softened and fragrant. Press Cancel.

6. Stir in the lemon juice. Return the squash strands to the pot and stir to coat. Stir in the Parmesan cheese and parsley. Season with the salt and pepper and serve.

Per serving (¼ recipe): Calories: 270; Fat: 19g; Protein: 6g; Total Carbs: 24g; Fiber: 5g; Sugar: 8g; Sodium: 322mg

Kung Pao Cauliflower

Kung pao chicken is one of my favorite things to order when we go out for Chinese food, but I also love making this healthier, plant-based version at home. Cauliflower is a great stand-in for chicken, and it absorbs so much flavor from the sauce. A sprinkle of chopped peanuts over the top gives this dish the perfect crunch.

SERVES 4

PREP TIME: 10 minutes

COOK SETTING: High Pressure for 2 minutes, then Sauté for 6 minutes

RELEASE: Quick

TOTAL TIME: 25 minutes

4 cups fresh cauliflower florets

1 teaspoon sesame oil

2 garlic cloves, minced

2 teaspoons red pepper flakes

¼ cup coconut aminos or tamari

2 tablespoons honey

⅛ teaspoon kosher salt

¼ cup peanuts, chopped

2 scallions, sliced, greens parts only

1. Pour ½ cup water into the Instant Pot and insert the trivet. Place the cauliflower on top of the trivet and lock the lid in place.

2. Select Manual or Pressure Cook and set the cooker to High Pressure for 2 minutes.

3. When the cook time is complete, quick release the pressure.

4. Carefully remove the lid and remove the cauliflower from the pot. Pour out any remaining water and wipe the pot dry.

5. Select Sauté on the Instant Pot and pour in the sesame oil. When the oil is hot, add the garlic and red pepper flakes. Cook for 1 to 2 minutes, stirring occasionally, until fragrant. Add the coconut aminos, honey, and salt. Cook for 3 to 4 minutes, stirring constantly, until reduced to a thick sauce. Press Cancel.

6. Return the cauliflower to the pot and stir to coat with sauce. Sprinkle with peanuts and scallions and serve.

SUBSTITUTION TIP: If you don't eat peanuts, swap them for cashews.

Per serving (¼ recipe): Calories: 136; Fat: 6g; Protein: 6g; Total Carbs: 17g; Fiber: 3g; Sugar: 12g; Sodium: 807mg

Sesame Peanut Soba Noodles

Soba noodles are made with buckwheat flour, which gives them a great nutty flavor. In this recipe, I combine them with broccoli slaw (a mixture of shredded broccoli, carrot, and cabbage that you can find premade in the produce section of the grocery store) and peanut sauce for an easy meal that's ready in just 10 minutes. Natural peanut butter can vary greatly in its salt content, so be sure to taste the final dish before deciding if you need to add more.

SERVES 4

PREP TIME: 5 minutes

COOK SETTING: High Pressure for 2 minutes

RELEASE: Quick

TOTAL TIME: 15 minutes

4 cups water

¼ cup coconut aminos or tamari

2 tablespoons sesame oil

1 (9.5-ounce) package soba noodles

12 ounces broccoli slaw mix

1 red bell pepper, seeded and sliced

¼ cup creamy natural peanut butter

½ teaspoon red pepper flakes

½ teaspoon kosher salt (optional)

1. In the Instant Pot, combine the water, coconut aminos, and sesame oil. Add the soba noodles, breaking them to fit in the pot if necessary. Press down on the noodles to submerge them. Top with the broccoli slaw and bell pepper. Lock the lid in place.

2. Select Manual or Pressure Cook and set the cooker to High Pressure for 2 minutes.

3. When the cook time is complete, quick release the pressure.

4. Carefully remove the lid and stir in the peanut butter and red pepper flakes. Season to taste with salt (if using) and serve.

SUBSTITUTION TIP: To make these noodles nut-free, use sunflower seed butter instead of peanut butter.

Per serving (¼ recipe): Calories: 430; Fat: 16g; Protein: 18g; Total Carbs: 62g; Fiber: 4g; Sugar: 4g; Sodium: 1021mg

Broccoli-Basil Pasta

This simple recipe is one of my go-to weeknight dinners. Fresh basil and minced garlic add tons of pesto-inspired flavor that the whole family will love. I use frozen broccoli for this recipe since it takes longer to cook than fresh broccoli does. This way, you can cook the broccoli at the same time as the pasta without it turning to mush.

SERVES 4

PREP TIME: 5 minutes

COOK SETTING: High Pressure for 2 minutes

RELEASE: Quick

TOTAL TIME: 20 minutes

8 ounces whole-grain or gluten-free penne

½ teaspoon kosher salt

2 cups water

3 cups frozen broccoli florets

1 cup fresh basil leaves, finely chopped

¼ cup olive oil

½ cup shredded Parmesan cheese

2 garlic cloves, minced

¼ teaspoon freshly ground black pepper

1. In the Instant Pot, combine the penne, salt, and water. Top with the broccoli. Lock the lid in place.

2. Select Manual or Pressure Cook and set the cooker to High Pressure for 2 minutes.

3. When the cook time is complete, quick release the pressure.

4. Carefully remove the lid and stir. Stir in the basil, olive oil, Parmesan, garlic, and pepper before serving.

VARIATION TIP: Transform this recipe into picnic-perfect pasta salad by adding ¼ cup of vinegar along with the other ingredients in step 4, then refrigerate until chilled.

Per serving (¼ recipe): Calories: 403; Fat: 18g; Protein: 15g; Total Carbs: 50g; Fiber: 8g; Sugar: 2g; Sodium: 345mg

Mushroom Stroganoff

Stroganoff is traditionally made with beef in a creamy, tangy sauce. For a vegetarian twist, I use portobello mushrooms. Be sure to use full-fat sour cream for this recipe, since low-fat variations can curdle.

SERVES 4

PREP TIME: 10 minutes

COOK SETTING: Sauté for 4 minutes, then High Pressure for 3 minutes

RELEASE: Quick

TOTAL TIME: 25 minutes

---

1 tablespoon olive oil

1 yellow onion, thinly sliced

3 garlic cloves, minced

1 pound portobello mushrooms, thinly sliced

1 tablespoon flour of choice

1¾ cups Vegetable Broth (page 116) or store-bought low-sodium vegetable broth

8 ounces whole-grain rotini pasta

1 tablespoon vegan Worcestershire sauce

2 tablespoons Dijon mustard

¾ teaspoon kosher salt

½ teaspoon whole black peppercorns

½ cup full-fat sour cream

1. Select Sauté on the Instant Pot and pour in the olive oil. When the oil is hot, add the onion and garlic and cook for 3 to 4 minutes, until softened. Add the mushrooms and flour and stir to combine. Press Cancel.

2. Add the broth, pasta, Worcestershire sauce, mustard, salt, and peppercorns. Stir to combine. Lock the lid in place.

3. Select Manual or Pressure Cook and set the cooker to High Pressure for 3 minutes.

4. When the cook time is complete, quick release the pressure.

5. Carefully remove the lid and stir in the sour cream before serving.

INGREDIENT TIP: Traditional Worcestershire sauce has anchovies in it, so be sure to look for a vegan version, such as Annie's Homegrown Organic and Vegan Worcestershire Sauce.

Per serving (¼ recipe): Calories: 337; Fat: 11g; Protein: 12g; Total Carbs: 54g; Fiber: 7g; Sugar: 5g; Sodium: 361mg

Vegetable Enchilada Casserole

Enchiladas are one of my favorite meals, but it takes forever to roll each tortilla. Layering the ingredients like a lasagna gives you that same great flavor but is so much easier. Cooking this enchilada casserole in a cake pan instead of directly in the Instant Pot helps prevent a burn warning.

SERVES 4

PREP TIME: 10 minutes

COOK SETTING: High Pressure for 15 minutes

RELEASE: Quick

TOTAL TIME: 40 minutes

2 cups baby spinach, chopped

2 cups shredded Cheddar cheese, divided

1 (15.5-ounce) can low-sodium black beans, drained and rinsed

4 scallions, white and light green parts, thinly sliced

1 cup frozen corn kernels

¼ cup water

¼ cup tomato paste

2 teaspoons ancho chili powder

¼ teaspoon salt

Nonstick cooking spray

6 corn tortillas

1. In a large bowl, combine the spinach, 1½ cups of cheese, the beans, scallions, corn, water, tomato paste, chili powder, and salt.

2. Grease a 6-inch cake pan with nonstick cooking spray.

3. Add 1 cup of the filling to the prepared pan and top it with a tortilla (if necessary, cut the tortilla to fit in your pan; it's okay if the pieces overlap a little). Repeat, alternating layers of filling and tortilla. Sprinkle the remaining ½ cup of cheese on top of the final layer. Do not cover.

4. Pour 1 cup of water into the Instant Pot and insert the trivet. Place the casserole on top of the trivet and lock the lid in place.

5. Select Manual or Pressure Cook and set the cooker to High Pressure for 15 minutes.

6. When the cook time is complete, quick release the pressure.

7. Carefully remove the lid and lift the casserole from the pot. Let it cool for 10 minutes, then cut into four portions and serve.

Per serving (1 slice): Calories: 463; Fat: 21g; Protein: 24g; Total Carbs: 46g; Fiber: 10g; Sugar: 4g; Sodium: 432mg

Arancini Casserole

Here, I've transformed arancini (Sicilian rice balls) into a hearty casserole that can be served as a meal. For added nutrition, I use a mixture of brown rice and cauliflower rice, but you'll never know the cauliflower is there from the taste. For the classic crunch of fried arancini, top the casserole with bread crumbs and broil for 2 to 3 minutes in the oven until crisp.

SERVES 6

PREP TIME: 5 minutes

COOK SETTING: Sauté for 4 minutes, then High Pressure for 20 minutes

RELEASE: Quick

TOTAL TIME: 40 minutes

1 tablespoon olive oil

1 yellow onion, diced

1 cup short-grain brown rice

1 cup frozen cauliflower rice

2 cups Marinara Sauce (page 118) or store-bought pasta sauce

1 cup water

2 cups shredded mozzarella

¼ cup panko bread crumbs (optional)

Olive oil spray (optional)

1. Select Sauté on the Instant Pot and pour in the olive oil. When the oil is hot, add the onion and cook for 3 to 4 minutes, stirring occasionally, until softened. Stir in the brown rice. Press Cancel.

2. Add the cauliflower rice, marinara, and water. Lock the lid in place.

3. Select Manual or Pressure Cook and set the cooker to High Pressure for 20 minutes.

4. When the cook time is complete, quick release the pressure.

5. Carefully remove the lid and stir the contents of the pot. Top the rice with the mozzarella, then replace the lid and let sit for 2 to 3 minutes, until the cheese has melted. Serve as is or proceed to step 6.

6. Preheat the oven to broil. Transfer the casserole to a small (9-by-6-inch) baking dish. Top it with a thin layer of panko bread crumbs and spritz with olive oil spray. Broil for 2 to 3 minutes, until toasted and golden brown. Cut into six slices and serve.

Per serving (⅙ recipe): Calories: 279; Fat: 12g; Protein: 12g; Total Carbs: 32g; Fiber: 3g; Sugar: 5g; Sodium: 250mg

Eggplant Parmesan

For this super-simple, lighter take on eggplant Parmesan, I skip the traditional step of breading and frying the eggplant before layering it with sauce and cheese. Eggplant comes out so tender and flavorful in the Instant Pot, you won't miss the breading. Adding water to the bottom of the pot will help prevent a burn warning, so don't skip that step!

SERVES 4

PREP TIME: 10 minutes

COOK SETTING: High Pressure for 10 minutes

RELEASE: Quick

TOTAL TIME: 30 minutes

---

2 medium eggplants

½ cup water

1½ cups Marinara Sauce (page 118) or store-bought pasta sauce

1 cup shredded mozzarella cheese

1. Cut the top and bottom off each eggplant, then slice the eggplants lengthwise into ¼-inch planks.

2. Pour the water into the Instant Pot. Stir in ½ cup of marinara sauce. Add two or three pieces of eggplant to form a single layer. Spread ½ cup of marinara sauce over the eggplant and sprinkle with ¼ cup of cheese. Repeat this process four times, ending with a cheese layer. Lock the lid in place.

3. Select Manual or Pressure Cook and set the cooker to High Pressure for 10 minutes.

4. When the cook time is complete, quick release the pressure.

5. Carefully remove the lid and serve.

SUBSTITUTION TIP: This recipe is also delicious made with layers of zucchini. You'll need about four large zucchini to replace the eggplant.

Per serving (¼ recipe): Calories: 175; Fat: 7g; Protein: 10g; Total Carbs: 22g; Fiber: 10g; Sugar: 13g; Sodium: 191mg

Lentil Sloppy Joe Lettuce Wraps

Lentils have a rich, meaty texture that makes them a great plant-based substitute for ground meat. I especially love using them in saucy recipes like these sloppy joes, which feature garden vegetables and a flavorful sauce. Because lentils are starchier than beef, I swap the traditional burger bun for lettuce leaves in which to wrap the filling. Lettuce provides a nice crunch and a fresh flavor that complements the savory filling. Depending on the size of the leaves and how much you fill each wrap, this recipe makes about 16 wraps.

SERVES 4

PREP TIME: 10 minutes

COOK SETTING: Sauté for 15 minutes, then High Pressure for 15 minutes

RELEASE: Natural

TOTAL TIME: 45 minutes

1 tablespoon olive oil

1 red onion, finely chopped

1 green bell pepper, seeded and finely chopped

1 zucchini, finely diced

2 carrots, peeled and finely diced

2 cups water

1 cup dried brown lentils

1 cup tomato sauce

1 teaspoon vegan Worcestershire sauce

1 teaspoon chili powder

Leaf lettuce, for serving

1. Select Sauté on the Instant Pot and pour in the olive oil. When the oil is hot, add the onion, bell pepper, zucchini, and carrots. Sauté for 5 to 6 minutes, until softened and lightly browned. Press Cancel.

2. Add the water, lentils, tomato sauce, Worcestershire sauce, and chili powder. Stir to combine. Lock the lid in place.

3. Select Manual or Pressure Cook and set the cooker to High Pressure for 15 minutes.

4. When the cook time is complete, let the pressure release naturally for 10 minutes, then quick release any remaining pressure.

5. Carefully remove the lid and stir the contents of the pot. If the sauce is too thin, select Sauté and simmer with the lid off for 5 to 10 minutes, until thickened. Serve the sloppy joe filling wrapped in lettuce leaves.

INGREDIENT TIP: Traditional Worcestershire sauce has anchovies in it, so be sure to look for a vegan version, such as Annie's Homegrown Organic and Vegan Worcestershire Sauce.

Per serving (¼ recipe): Calories: 254; Fat: 4g; Protein: 14g; Total Carbs: 43g; Fiber: 9g; Sugar: 8g; Sodium: 70mg

Chapter 5

Fish and Poultry

Shrimp Boil
PAGE 72

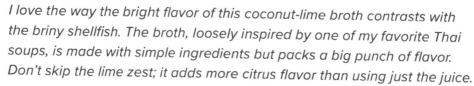

Coconut-Lime Mussels

I love the way the bright flavor of this coconut-lime broth contrasts with the briny shellfish. The broth, loosely inspired by one of my favorite Thai soups, is made with simple ingredients but packs a big punch of flavor. Don't skip the lime zest; it adds more citrus flavor than using just the juice.

SERVES 4

PREP TIME: 5 minutes, plus 15 minutes to soak

COOK SETTING: High Pressure for 3 minutes

RELEASE: Quick

TOTAL TIME: 35 minutes

1 (13.5-ounce) can full-fat unsweetened coconut milk

2 cups water

1 (1-inch) knob fresh ginger, grated

Zest and juice of 1 lime

3 pounds fresh mussels, soaked and scrubbed

¼ cup fresh cilantro, chopped

1. In the Instant Pot, combine the coconut milk, water, ginger, lime zest, and lime juice. Stir well. Add the mussels to the pot and lock the lid in place.

2. Select Manual or Pressure Cook and set the cooker to High Pressure for 3 minutes.

3. When the cook time is complete, quick release the pressure.

4. Carefully remove the lid and stir in the cilantro before serving.

INGREDIENT TIP: Mussels live in sand, so it's important to let them soak in cold water for 15 minutes and give them a gentle scrub before you cook them. Otherwise, they can be gritty. Prior to cooking, discard any mussels that are open or have broken shells. Discard any mussels that remain unopened after cooking.

Per serving (¼ recipe): Calories: 264; Fat: 22g; Protein: 12g; Total Carbs: 7g; Fiber: 0g; Sugar: 0g; Sodium: 256mg

Seafood Cioppino

Cioppino is a rich seafood stew hailing from San Francisco. Traditionally made with whatever the fishermen brought in that day, fish and shellfish infuses the tomato-based broth with tons of flavor.

SERVES 6

PREP TIME: 10 minutes

COOK SETTING: Sauté for 4 minutes, then High Pressure for 3 minutes

RELEASE: Natural

TOTAL TIME: 30 minutes

1 tablespoon olive oil

1 yellow onion, finely chopped

2 garlic cloves, thinly sliced

1 pound firm, skinless white fish (such as halibut), cut into 1-inch pieces

1 pound large shrimp

1 pound littleneck clams

2 cups Marinara Sauce (page 118) or store-bought marinara

1½ cups low-sodium seafood stock

2 celery stalks, finely chopped

1 green bell pepper, seeded and finely chopped

1 teaspoon dried oregano

1. Select Sauté on the Instant Pot and pour in the olive oil. When the oil is hot, add the onion and garlic. Cook for 3 to 4 minutes, stirring occasionally, until softened. Press Cancel.

2. Add the white fish, shrimp, clams, marinara sauce, seafood stock, celery, bell pepper, and oregano. Lock the lid in place.

3. Select Manual or Pressure Cook and set the cooker to High Pressure for 3 minutes.

4. When the cook time is complete, let the pressure release naturally for 5 minutes, then quick release any remaining pressure.

5. Carefully remove the lid and serve.

VARIATION TIP: For this recipe, I used a combination of white fish, shrimp, and clams, but you can use any combination of fish or shellfish you like. Mussels, calamari, and scallops are all nice additions and won't require an adjustment to this recipe's cook time.

Per serving (⅙ recipe): Calories: 186; Fat: 4g; Protein: 27g; Total Carbs: 9g; Fiber: 2g; Sugar: 4g; Sodium: 463mg

Shrimp Boil

Some of my favorite memories involve sitting outside in the summer and eating shrimp boil. It's so fast and easy to make in the Instant Pot. I give the potatoes a head start so they can get nice and tender, then I add frozen shrimp right at the end of the cooking process so they don't over-cook and get tough. If you're using fresh shrimp, shorten the cook time in step 2 to 1 minute.

SERVES 4

PREP TIME: 5 minutes

COOK SETTING: High Pressure for 7 minutes

RELEASE: Quick

TOTAL TIME: 20 minutes

1 cup Chicken Stock (page 115) or store-bought low-sodium chicken stock

1 pound baby red potatoes, halved

4 links all-natural Cajun-style sausage, sliced

4 ears fresh corn, shucked and halved crosswise

1 tablespoon Cajun seasoning

1 pound frozen peel-and-eat shrimp

¼ cup fresh parsley, chopped

1 lemon, cut into wedges

1. In the Instant Pot, combine the stock, potatoes, sausage, corn, and Cajun seasoning. Lock the lid in place.

2. Select Manual or Pressure Cook and set the cooker to High Pressure for 5 minutes.

3. When the cook time is complete, quick release the pressure.

4. Carefully remove the lid and add the shrimp. Lock the lid in place. Select Manual or Pressure Cook and set the cooker to High Pressure for 2 minutes. When the cook time is complete, quick release the pressure.

5. Carefully remove the lid and stir in the parsley. Serve with lemon wedges.

SUBSTITUTION TIP: For a pescatarian version of this recipe, use 2 pounds of shrimp, omit the sausage, and swap the chicken stock for Vegetable Broth (page 116) or store-bought low-sodium vegetable broth.

Per serving (¼ recipe): Calories: 615; Fat: 31g; Protein: 42g; Total Carbs: 46g; Fiber: 6g; Sugar: 6g; Sodium: 744mg

Lemon and Dill Tilapia

Cooking fish at home can be intimidating, but the Instant Pot makes it so easy. Tilapia fillets straight from the freezer come out perfectly tender and flaky. I love keeping a bag of them on hand for when I want an easy meal that isn't chicken or beef. Be sure to use parchment paper for this recipe. Aluminum foil will insulate the fish too well and require a much longer cook time.

SERVES 4

PREP TIME: 10 minutes

COOK SETTING: High Pressure for 17 minutes

RELEASE: Quick

TOTAL TIME: 35 minutes

2 medium zucchini, sliced

4 (4-ounce) frozen tilapia fillets

1 lemon, cut into 8 slices

1 teaspoon butter

2 tablespoons freshly chopped dill

1. Place a sheet of parchment paper on your counter. Position one-quarter of the zucchini slices in the center of the parchment and top them with 1 tilapia fillet, 2 lemon slices, ¼ teaspoon of butter, and ½ tablespoon of dill. Fold the parchment over the fish and crimp the edges to create a sealed packet. Repeat three times for a total of four packets.

2. Pour 1 cup of water into the Instant Pot and insert the trivet. Stack the packets on top of the trivet. Lock the lid in place.

3. Select Manual or Pressure Cook and set the cooker to High Pressure for 17 minutes.

4. When the cook time is complete, quick release the pressure.

5. Carefully remove the lid and remove the packets from the pot. Unfold the parchment and serve.

SUBSTITUTION TIP: I love the flavor that a little bit of butter gives this recipe, but for a dairy-free version, replace it with a drizzle of olive oil.

Per serving (1 packet): Calories: 137; Fat: 3g; Protein: 24g; Total Carbs: 4g; Fiber: 1g; Sugar: 3g; Sodium: 75mg

Maple-Mustard Salmon with Asparagus

You won't believe how easy it is to cook salmon in the Instant Pot. It comes out succulent and flaky with just 3 minutes under pressure. Because adding the asparagus at the beginning cooks it too much, you'll interrupt the cook time to add the asparagus to the pot. But don't worry, your Instant Pot will return to pressure quickly. If you want, caramelize the glaze by broiling the salmon for 1 minute in the oven before serving.

SERVES 4

PREP TIME: 10 minutes

COOK SETTING: High Pressure for 3 minutes

RELEASE: Quick

TOTAL TIME: 20 minutes

1 tablespoon pure maple syrup

1 tablespoon Dijon mustard

⅛ teaspoon kosher salt

4 (6-ounce) salmon fillets

1 pound asparagus, trimmed

1 cup cherry tomatoes, halved

INGREDIENT TIP: It's important that your salmon fillets measure between ¾ and 1 inch thick; otherwise, they might overcook.

1. In a small bowl, combine the maple syrup, mustard, and salt. Spread the sauce onto the salmon fillets.

2. Pour 1 cup of water into the Instant Pot and insert the trivet. Place the salmon fillets on the trivet. Lock the lid in place.

3. Select Manual or Pressure Cook and set the cooker to High Pressure for 2 minutes.

4. When the cook time is complete, quick release the pressure.

5. Carefully remove the lid and add the asparagus. Lock the lid in place. Select Manual or Pressure Cook and set the cooker to High Pressure for 1 minute. When the cook time is complete, quick release the pressure.

6. Carefully remove the lid. Remove the asparagus from the pot and mix it with the tomatoes. Serve alongside the salmon.

Per serving (1 salmon fillet and ¼ vegetables): Calories: 286; Fat: 11g; Protein: 37g; Total Carbs: 9g; Fiber: 3g; Sugar: 6g; Sodium: 161mg

Balsamic Chicken

Balsamic chicken is one of the most popular recipes on my website, so I knew I needed to develop a clean eating Instant Pot version for this book. I love how quickly this comes together. Carrots nicely highlight the sweetness of the balsamic vinegar, and potatoes round out the meal. If you prefer, leave the potatoes out and serve this recipe with Cauliflower Mashed Potatoes (page 47) instead.

SERVES 4

PREP TIME: 5 minutes

COOK SETTING: High Pressure for 8 minutes

RELEASE: Natural

TOTAL TIME: 30 minutes

¼ cup Chicken Stock (page 115) or store-bought low-sodium chicken stock

2 tablespoons balsamic vinegar

4 garlic cloves, minced

1½ pounds chicken tenderloins

1 pound baby red potatoes

8 carrots, peeled and cut into thirds

½ teaspoon cornstarch

¼ teaspoon kosher salt

¼ teaspoon freshly ground black pepper

1. In the Instant Pot, combine the stock, vinegar, and garlic. Stir well. Add the chicken, potatoes, and carrots. Lock the lid in place.

2. Select Manual or Pressure Cook and set the cooker to High Pressure for 8 minutes.

3. When the cook time is complete, let the pressure release naturally for 10 minutes, then quick release any remaining pressure.

4. Carefully remove the lid and transfer the chicken and vegetables to a serving dish, leaving the juices behind.

5. Select Sauté. Whisk in the cornstarch and simmer for 2 to 3 minutes, until thickened. Season with the salt and pepper. Spoon the sauce over the chicken and vegetables to serve.

SUBSTITUTION TIP: To make this meal grain-free, thicken the sauce with arrowroot powder instead of cornstarch.

Per serving (¼ recipe): Calories: 336; Fat: 3g; Protein: 43g; Total Carbs: 32g; Fiber: 5g; Sugar: 8g; Sodium: 265mg

Chicken Tikka Masala

The Instant Pot cooks chicken breast quickly without drying it out, making it perfect for quick curries like this one. Curries are traditionally finished with heavy cream or coconut milk, but I love the convenience of using plain yogurt. Serve this recipe over brown rice or keep things grain-free with cauliflower rice.

SERVES 4

PREP TIME: 5 minutes

COOK SETTING: High Pressure for 13 minutes

RELEASE: Natural

TOTAL TIME: 35 minutes

1 pound boneless, skinless chicken breast, cubed

1 cup tomato puree

¼ cup water

1 yellow onion, chopped

4 garlic cloves, minced

1 (1-inch) knob fresh ginger, grated

1 tablespoon garam masala

¼ teaspoon kosher salt

¼ cup Homemade Yogurt (page 121) or store-bought plain whole-milk yogurt

1 cup frozen peas

1. In the Instant Pot, combine the chicken, tomato puree, water, onion, garlic, ginger, garam masala, and salt. Lock the lid in place.

2. Select Manual or Pressure Cook and set the cooker to High Pressure for 13 minutes.

3. When the cook time is complete, let the pressure release naturally for 10 minutes, then quick release any remaining pressure.

4. Carefully remove the lid and stir in the yogurt and peas. Let sit for 1 to 2 minutes, until the peas are warmed through, then serve.

SUBSTITUTION TIP: For a vegetarian version of this dish, substitute 2 (15.5-ounce) cans of chickpeas (drained) in place of the chicken. Use a quick release in step 3.

Per serving (¼ recipe): Calories: 189; Fat: 3g; Protein: 29g; Total Carbs: 12g; Fiber: 3g; Sugar: 6g; Sodium: 187mg

Chicken Fajitas

The Instant Pot makes fajita night easier than ever. The bell peppers and onions release a lot of liquid as they cook, so there's no need for any additional water or broth. Steaming the chicken on top of the vegetables keeps it away from the bottom of the pot, preventing a burn warning. The chicken and pepper mixture is packed with flavor on its own, but you can top these fajitas with cilantro, Restaurant-Style Salsa (page 117), or sour cream if you like.

SERVES 4

PREP TIME: 10 minutes

COOK SETTING: High Pressure for 12 minutes

RELEASE: Natural

TOTAL TIME: 35 minutes

2 red or yellow bell peppers, seeded and sliced

1 red onion, sliced

1 teaspoon olive oil

½ teaspoon chili powder

¼ teaspoon kosher salt

1¼ pounds boneless, skinless chicken breast, thinly sliced

12 cassava flour or corn tortillas

1. In the Instant Pot, combine the bell peppers, onion, olive oil, chili powder, and salt. Place the chicken slices on top of the vegetables. Lock the lid in place.

2. Select Manual or Pressure Cook and set the cooker to High Pressure for 12 minutes.

3. When the cook time is complete, let the pressure release naturally for 5 minutes, then quick release any remaining pressure.

4. Carefully remove the lid. Use a slotted spoon to divide the filling evenly across the tortillas, leaving any liquid in the pot.

SUBSTITUTION TIP: If you're lucky enough to have access to fresh, whole jicama, it makes a great substitute for tortillas when sliced thinly on a mandoline.

Per serving (3 fajitas): Calories: 367; Fat: 7g; Protein: 37g; Total Carbs: 38g; Fiber: 6g; Sugar: 4g; Sodium: 187mg

Chicken Cacciatore

Chicken cacciatore is an earthy, tomato-based stew that features chicken, mushrooms, and olives. Traditionally, this dish is slowly braised in the oven, but the Instant Pot delivers maximum flavor in a fraction of the time. This stew can be served on its own or with Cauliflower Mashed Potatoes (page 47) or soft polenta for a heartier meal.

SERVES 6

PREP TIME: 10 minutes

COOK SETTING: Sauté for 8 minutes, then High Pressure for 12 minutes

RELEASE: Natural

TOTAL TIME: 50 minutes

6 bone-in chicken thighs, with skin

¼ teaspoon kosher salt

¼ teaspoon freshly ground black pepper

2 tablespoons olive oil

1 (28-ounce) can crushed tomatoes

2 green bell peppers, seeded and diced

1 pint cremini mushrooms, halved lengthwise

½ cup pitted black olives

1 yellow onion, diced

1 teaspoon dried oregano

2 garlic cloves, minced

1 teaspoon balsamic vinegar

1. Season the chicken with the salt and black pepper.

2. Select Sauté on the Instant Pot and pour in the olive oil. When the oil is hot, add the chicken, skin-side down. Cook undisturbed for 5 to 8 minutes, until the skin is golden brown. Turn the chicken so it's skin-side up. Press Cancel.

3. Add the tomatoes, bell peppers, mushrooms, olives, onion, oregano, garlic, and balsamic vinegar to the Instant Pot. Lock the lid in place.

4. Select Manual or Pressure Cook and set the cooker to High Pressure for 12 minutes.

5. When the cook time is complete, let the pressure release naturally for 10 minutes, then quick release any remaining pressure.

6. Carefully remove the lid and serve.

SUBSTITUTION TIP: Bone-in, skin-on chicken thighs give this recipe the best flavor, but you can make it with boneless, skinless chicken breasts if you prefer. Shorten the cook time in step 4 to 8 minutes to keep the chicken breasts from overcooking.

Per serving (1 chicken thigh and ⅙ vegetable mixture): Calories: 520; Fat: 38g; Protein: 34g; Total Carbs: 10g; Fiber: 4g; Sugar: 5g; Sodium: 446mg

Basil Chicken with Green Beans

This tasty chicken dish is inspired by one of my favorite Thai restaurants. Ground chicken is enhanced by the mouthwatering sauce, and steamed fresh green beans provide a nice, crisp texture. You can enjoy this recipe as written or, for a more substantial meal, serve it with a side of brown rice.

SERVES 4

PREP TIME: 5 minutes

COOK SETTING: Sauté for 3 minutes, then High Pressure for 2 minutes

RELEASE: Quick

TOTAL TIME: 20 minutes

2 teaspoons olive oil

1½ pounds ground chicken

1 red bell pepper, seeded and sliced

1 shallot, finely chopped

1 tablespoon all-natural chile pepper paste

½ cup water

1 tablespoon coconut aminos or tamari

1 tablespoon gluten-free fish sauce

½ pound fresh green beans

1 cup whole fresh basil leaves

1. Select Sauté on the Instant Pot and pour in the olive oil. When the oil is hot, add the chicken and cook for 2 to 3 minutes to brown, stirring occasionally to break up the meat. Press Cancel.

2. Add the bell pepper, shallot, chile pepper paste, water, coconut aminos, and fish sauce. Stir to combine. Lock the lid in place.

3. Select Manual or Pressure Cook and set the cooker to High Pressure for 2 minutes.

4. When the cook time is complete, quick release the pressure.

5. Carefully remove the lid and add the green beans. Select Keep Warm, return the lid to the pot, and let it sit for 5 minutes, until the green beans are steamed. Remove the lid and stir in the basil before serving.

VARIATION TIP: Switch things up by using ground pork or ground turkey instead of ground chicken.

Per serving (¼ recipe): Calories: 298; Fat: 16g; Protein: 32g; Total Carbs: 7g; Fiber: 2g; Sugar: 4g; Sodium: 513mg

Greek-Inspired Chicken and Quinoa

I'm absolutely obsessed with quinoa's sweet, nutty flavor. Before cooking this tasty seed, it's important to rinse it until the water runs clear. This washes away the saponin, a naturally bitter substance that coats the seeds to deter birds from eating it in the wild (it can also upset your stomach). Most quinoa at the grocery store comes prerinsed, but it's best to rinse it again.

SERVES 4

PREP TIME: 5 minutes

COOK SETTING: Sauté for 4 minutes, then High Pressure for 10 minutes

RELEASE: Natural

TOTAL TIME: 35 minutes

2 tablespoons olive oil

1 red onion, finely chopped

1 red bell pepper, seeded and finely chopped

1 cup Chicken Stock (page 115) or store-bought low-sodium chicken stock

1½ pounds boneless, skinless chicken breast, cubed

¾ cup quinoa, rinsed well

1 teaspoon dried oregano

½ teaspoon kosher salt

1. Select Sauté on the Instant Pot and pour in the olive oil. When the oil is hot, add the onion and bell pepper. Cook for 3 to 4 minutes, stirring occasionally, until softened. Press Cancel.

2. Add the stock, chicken, quinoa, oregano, salt, and black pepper. Lock the lid in place.

3. Select Manual or Pressure Cook and set the cooker to High Pressure for 10 minutes.

4. When the cook time is complete, let the pressure release naturally for 10 minutes, then quick release any remaining pressure.

½ teaspoon freshly ground black pepper

1 cup grape or cherry tomatoes, halved

½ cup pitted kala-mata olives

¼ cup crumbled full-fat feta cheese

2 tablespoons freshly squeezed lemon juice

5. Carefully remove the lid and stir in the tomatoes, olives, feta, and lemon juice before serving.

SUBSTITUTION TIP: For a vegan variation on this dish, swap 1 (15.5-ounce) can of chickpeas or white beans for the chicken and omit the feta.

Per serving (¼ recipe): Calories: 454; Fat: 17g; Protein: 45g; Total Carbs: 28g; Fiber: 4g; Sugar: 4g; Sodium: 437mg

Turkey Lettuce Wraps

With so many contrasting flavors and textures, lettuce wraps are super fun to eat! For this recipe, I swapped the traditional ground chicken for more flavorful ground turkey. Use 93 percent lean ground turkey—which is less greasy than 85 or 90 percent lean versions—but stay away from 99 percent lean turkey breast, which can be dry.

SERVES 4

PREP TIME: 5 minutes

COOK SETTING: Sauté for 3 minutes, then High Pressure for 5 minutes

RELEASE: Natural

TOTAL TIME: 30 minutes

1 tablespoon olive oil

1 yellow onion, diced

2 garlic cloves, minced

1 pound lean (93 percent) ground turkey

⅓ cup water

2 tablespoons honey

2 tablespoons coconut aminos or tamari

1 tablespoon rice vinegar

1 (1-inch) knob fresh ginger, grated

1 (8-ounce) can water chestnuts, drained and diced

2 scallions, white and light green parts, thinly sliced

1 head butter lettuce

1. Select Sauté on the Instant Pot and pour in the olive oil. When the oil is hot, add the onion and garlic and cook for 2 to 3 minutes, stirring occasionally, until softened. Press Cancel.

2. Add the ground turkey, water, honey, coconut aminos, vinegar, and ginger. Stir well to break up the meat. Lock the lid in place.

3. Select Manual or Pressure Cook and set the cooker to High Pressure for 5 minutes.

4. When the cook time is complete, let the pressure release naturally for 10 minutes, then quick release any remaining pressure.

5. Carefully remove the lid and stir in the water chestnuts and scallions. If the sauce is too thin, select Keep Warm and simmer, uncovered, for 3 to 4 minutes, until thickened. Serve with lettuce for wrapping.

SUBSTITUTION TIP: For a vegetarian take on this dish, use 12 to 14 ounces of extra-firm tofu instead of the turkey. Shorten the cook time in step 3 to 3 minutes, then quick release the pressure.

Per serving (¼ recipe): Calories: 355; Fat: 13g; Protein: 25g; Total Carbs: 35g; Fiber: 1g; Sugar: 10g; Sodium: 488mg

Turkey Dinner

Did you know you can cook a turkey dinner in your Instant Pot? This turkey, complete with vegetables inspired by the flavor of stuffing, is ready in under an hour. Giving the turkey a 20-minute head start in the Instant Pot before adding the vegetables means everything finishes cooking at the same time. If desired, you can make a simple gravy by whisking 1 tablespoon of cornstarch into the liquid at the bottom of the pan before serving.

SERVES 4

PREP TIME: 10 minutes

COOK SETTING: High Pressure for 30 minutes

RELEASE: Quick, then Natural

TOTAL TIME: 1 hour

1½ pounds turkey tenderloin

2 teaspoons olive oil, divided

½ teaspoon poultry seasoning

½ teaspoon kosher salt

¼ teaspoon freshly ground black pepper

2 cups cubed butternut squash

4 celery stalks, sliced

4 carrots, peeled and sliced

1. Coat the turkey with 1 teaspoon of olive oil, then sprinkle it with the poultry seasoning, salt, and pepper. Set aside.

2. Place the squash, celery, and carrots on a piece of aluminum foil. Bring the sides of the foil up like a boat to contain the vegetables, but do not cover the top. Drizzle the vegetables with the remaining 1 teaspoon of olive oil, then set aside.

3. Pour 1 cup of water into the Instant Pot and insert the trivet. Place the turkey on top of the trivet and lock the lid in place.

4. Select Manual or Pressure Cook and set the cooker to High Pressure for 20 minutes.

5. When the cook time is complete, quick release the pressure.

6. Carefully remove the lid and place the foil packet of vegetables directly on top of the turkey. Lock the lid in place.

CONTINUED

7. Select Manual or Pressure Cook and set the cooker to High Pressure for 10 minutes.

8. When the cook time is complete, let the pressure release naturally for 10 minutes, then quick release any remaining pressure.

9. Carefully remove the lid and lift out the foil packet of vegetables. Transfer the turkey to a cutting board and slice it before serving alongside the vegetables.

VARIATION TIP: Feel free to get creative with the vegetables you use in this recipe. Sturdy vegetables like diced sweet potatoes or Brussels sprouts are great options that will cook in the same amount of time as those used here. More delicate options, such as green beans, will cook faster.

Per serving (¼ recipe): Calories: 281; Fat: 7g; Protein: 41g; Total Carbs: 16g; Fiber: 4g; Sugar: 5g; Sodium: 367mg

Beef, Pork, and Lamb

Green Curry Pork
PAGE 97

Beef and Broccoli

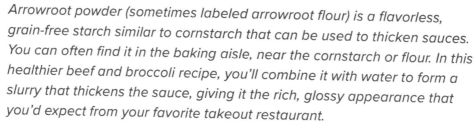

Arrowroot powder (sometimes labeled arrowroot flour) is a flavorless, grain-free starch similar to cornstarch that can be used to thicken sauces. You can often find it in the baking aisle, near the cornstarch or flour. In this healthier beef and broccoli recipe, you'll combine it with water to form a slurry that thickens the sauce, giving it the rich, glossy appearance that you'd expect from your favorite takeout restaurant.

SERVES 6

PREP TIME: 10 minutes

COOK SETTING: High Pressure for 10 minutes

RELEASE: Natural

TOTAL TIME: 35 minutes

1 tablespoon arrow-
   root powder

1 tablespoon water,
   plus ¼ cup

2 tablespoons sesame oil

2 tablespoons coconut
   aminos or tamari

4 garlic cloves, minced

1 (1-inch) knob fresh
   ginger, grated

2 pounds flank steak, cut
   into 1-inch slices

6 cups fresh broc-
   coli florets

1. In a small bowl, whisk together the arrowroot powder and 1 tablespoon of water. Set aside.

2. In the Instant Pot, combine the sesame oil, coconut aminos, garlic, ginger, and ¼ cup of water. Add the steak slices and stir to coat. Layer the broccoli on top of the steak. Lock the lid in place.

3. Select Manual or Pressure Cook and set the cooker to High Pressure for 10 minutes.

4. When the cook time is complete, let the pressure release naturally for 10 minutes, then quick release any remaining pressure.

5. Carefully remove the lid and stir in the arrowroot slurry. Let the beef and broccoli sit for 1 to 2 minutes to thicken before serving.

INGREDIENT TIP: Looking at the raw steak, you'll notice long fibers running lengthwise along the steak. Slice the steak perpendicular to these fibers (against the grain), cutting them into short pieces. Cutting parallel to the fibers can result in steak that's very tough and chewy.

Per serving (⅙ recipe): Calories: 290; Fat: 12g; Protein: 36g; Total Carbs: 8g; Fiber: 3g; Sugar: 2g; Sodium: 346mg

Beef and Bean Chili

When fall arrives, I start craving this beef and bean chili. Before getting my first Instant Pot, I'd simmer it on the stove all afternoon. Now I can get that same delicious dish in just 30 minutes. Crushed tomatoes give this chili a thick sauce without an overwhelming tomato flavor. If you can find them, fire-roasted crushed tomatoes provide an extra layer of smoky flavor that I love.

SERVES 6

PREP TIME: 5 minutes

COOK SETTING: Sauté for 8 minutes, then High Pressure for 10 minutes

RELEASE: Natural

TOTAL TIME: 40 minutes

1 tablespoon olive oil

1 yellow onion, diced

2 pounds lean (93 percent) ground beef

1 (28-ounce) can crushed tomatoes, preferably fire-roasted

1 (15.5-ounce) can red kidney beans, drained and rinsed

1 green bell pepper, seeded and chopped

2 tablespoons chili powder

½ teaspoon smoked paprika

¼ teaspoon kosher salt

¼ teaspoon cayenne pepper (optional)

1. Select Sauté on the Instant Pot and pour in the olive oil. When the oil is hot, add the onion. Cook for 3 to 4 minutes, stirring frequently, until softened. Add the beef and cook for another 2 to 4 minutes, using a wooden spoon to break it up. Press Cancel.

2. Add the crushed tomatoes, kidney beans, bell pepper, chili powder, paprika, salt, and cayenne pepper (if using). Stir well. Lock the lid in place.

3. Select Manual or Pressure Cook and set the cooker to High Pressure for 10 minutes.

4. When the cook time is complete, let the pressure release naturally for 10 minutes, then quick release any remaining pressure.

5. Carefully remove the lid and serve.

SUBSTITUTION TIP: For a vegetarian chili, omit the beef and add another can of kidney beans along with 1 (15.5-ounce) can of black beans.

Per serving (⅙ recipe): Calories: 313; Fat: 11g; Protein: 38g; Total Carbs: 19g; Fiber: 8g; Sugar: 5g; Sodium: 383mg

Beef Stew with Parsnips

I love adding parsnips to my stew along with the carrots and potatoes. They have a slightly peppery, earthy flavor that's really unique. Once you've tried them, you'll never want to make stew any other way!

SERVES 6

PREP TIME: 10 minutes

COOK SETTING: Sauté for 4 minutes, then High Pressure for 35 minutes

RELEASE: Natural

TOTAL TIME: 1 hour 20 minutes

2 pounds beef stew meat, cubed

½ teaspoon kosher salt

¼ teaspoon freshly ground black pepper

2 tablespoons olive oil

1½ pounds small white potatoes, quartered

4 carrots, peeled and cut into 1-inch pieces

2 parsnips, peeled and cut into 1-inch pieces

1 yellow onion, chopped

4 garlic cloves, minced

1 cup low-sodium beef broth

1 (6-ounce) can tomato paste

8 thyme sprigs

1½ cups frozen peas

1. Use a paper towel to pat the beef dry, then season it with the salt and pepper.

2. Select Sauté on the Instant Pot and pour in the oil. When the oil is hot, add the beef cubes and cook, undisturbed, for 3 to 4 minutes, until browned on the bottom. Press Cancel.

3. Stir in the potatoes, carrots, parsnips, onion, garlic, broth, and tomato paste. Place the thyme on top of the other ingredients. Lock the lid in place.

4. Select Manual or Pressure Cook and set the cooker to High Pressure for 35 minutes.

5. When the cook time is complete, let the pressure release naturally for 15 minutes, then quick release any remaining pressure.

6. Carefully remove the lid and remove the thyme stems. Stir in the peas. Let sit for 2 to 3 minutes, or until the peas are warmed through, and serve.

INGREDIENT TIP: Cutting the carrots and parsnips into big pieces keeps them from breaking down and disintegrating in your stew. You can use your thumb as a measuring guide; 1 inch is roughly the length from knuckle to fingertip.

Per serving (⅙ recipe): Calories: 419; Fat: 11g; Protein: 39g; Total Carbs: 43g; Fiber: 9g; Sugar: 12g; Sodium: 327mg

Beef and Barley Soup

This is without a doubt the best beef and barley soup I've ever tasted. The broth is incredibly rich, and the beef is so tender that it practically melts in your mouth. Fresh parsley stirred in before serving brightens it up. I also like to add more freshly ground black pepper directly to my bowl.

SERVES 4

PREP TIME: 10 minutes

COOK SETTING: High Pressure for 30 minutes

RELEASE: Natural

TOTAL TIME: 1 hour

4 cups low-sodium beef broth

1 pound beef chuck roast, cut into ¾-inch pieces

¾ cup barley

2 carrots, peeled and chopped

2 celery stalks, chopped

1 yellow onion, diced

4 garlic cloves, minced

2 tablespoons double concentrated tomato paste

¾ teaspoon kosher salt

½ teaspoon freshly ground black pepper

¼ cup fresh parsley, chopped

1. In the Instant Pot, combine the broth, beef, barley, carrots, celery, onion, garlic, tomato paste, salt, and pepper. Lock the lid in place.

2. Select Manual or Pressure Cook and set the cooker to High Pressure for 30 minutes.

3. When the cook time is complete, let the pressure release naturally for 10 minutes, then quick release any remaining pressure.

4. Carefully remove the lid and stir in the parsley.

SUBSTITUTION TIP: For a gluten-free option, substitute buckwheat groats for the barley.

Per serving (¼ recipe): Calories: 327; Fat: 7g; Protein: 29g; Total Carbs: 39g; Fiber: 9g; Sugar: 5g; Sodium: 374mg

Garlicky Steak Bites

The next time you're craving steak and potatoes, look no further than your Instant Pot. Savory bites of sirloin steak come out so tender when cooked under pressure. I also add cremini mushrooms to enhance the steak's rich flavor. Cut the mushrooms into quarters so they're roughly the same size as the steak bites. That way, each forkful will be perfectly balanced.

SERVES 4

PREP TIME: 10 minutes

COOK SETTING: Sauté for 4 minutes, then High Pressure for 10 minutes

RELEASE: Natural

TOTAL TIME: 40 minutes

1½ pounds sirloin steak, cut into 1-inch cubes

⅛ teaspoon kosher salt

⅛ teaspoon freshly ground black pepper

2 tablespoons olive oil

4 garlic cloves, minced

½ cup low-sodium beef broth

1 pound baby yellow potatoes

1 pint cremini mushrooms, quartered

1. Use a paper towel to pat the steak dry, then season it with the salt and pepper.

2. Select Sauté on the Instant Pot and pour in the olive oil. When the oil is hot, add the steak cubes, working in batches if necessary to avoid crowding the pan. Cook for 3 to 4 minutes, stirring occasionally, until all sides are browned. Stir in the garlic. Press Cancel.

3. Pour in the broth and scrape up any browned bits from the bottom of the pot. Add the potatoes and mushrooms. Lock the lid in place.

4. Select Manual or Pressure Cook and set the cooker to High Pressure for 10 minutes.

5. When the cook time is complete, let the pressure release naturally for 10 minutes, then quick release any remaining pressure.

6. Carefully remove the lid and serve.

FLAVOR BOOST: Sprinkle on some fresh parsley before serving for a pop of fresh flavor.

Per serving (¼ recipe): Calories: 477; Fat: 26g; Protein: 38g; Total Carbs: 21g; Fiber: 3g; Sugar: 1g; Sodium: 137mg

Stuffed Peppers

Stuffed peppers are a classic meal that's full of nostalgia for so many people. Making them in the Instant Pot is so easy, and I love that you don't need to fuss with a water bath like you do when making them in the oven. This recipe is a great way to use up any leftover brown rice that you might have hanging out in the refrigerator.

SERVES 4

PREP TIME: 10 minutes

COOK SETTING: High Pressure for 10 minutes

RELEASE: Natural

TOTAL TIME: 40 minutes

4 red or orange bell peppers

1 pound lean (93 percent) ground beef

1 cup Marinara Sauce (page 118) or store-bought marinara sauce

1 cup cooked brown rice

1 tablespoon Italian seasoning

½ teaspoon kosher salt

¼ cup shredded mozzarella cheese

1. Cut the top off each pepper and remove the seeds; set aside.

2. In a large bowl, combine the ground beef, marinara sauce, brown rice, Italian seasoning, and salt. Spoon the filling evenly into the peppers (if you have enough of the beef mixture, fill them to the top).

3. Pour 1 cup of water into the Instant Pot and insert the trivet. Arrange the peppers, filling-side up, on the trivet. Lock the lid in place.

4. Select Manual or Pressure Cook and set the cooker to High Pressure for 10 minutes.

5. When the cook time is complete, let the pressure release naturally for 10 minutes, then quick release any remaining pressure.

6. Carefully remove the lid and top the stuffed peppers with mozzarella. Replace the lid and let the peppers steam for 3 to 4 minutes to melt the cheese.

SUBSTITUTION TIP: To make these grain-free, use 1 cup of cauliflower rice instead of the brown rice. You can also use a mixture of half rice and half cauliflower rice.

Per serving (1 pepper): Calories: 276; Fat: 8g; Protein: 29g; Total Carbs: 22g; Fiber: 4g; Sugar: 7g; Sodium: 276mg

Spaghetti and Meatballs

Whenever I get my choice of a special meal, I always pick homemade meatballs. Mixing the meat and rolling it into balls will always be a labor of love, but the Instant Pot makes cooking them so much faster. While they only take a few minutes to cook, their flavors infuse into the sauce as if they had cooked all day long.

SERVES 4

PREP TIME: 20 minutes

COOK SETTING: Sauté for 8 minutes, then High Pressure for 3 minutes

RELEASE: Natural

TOTAL TIME: 50 minutes

1 pound lean (93 percent) ground beef

1 cup whole-wheat bread crumbs

1 egg, beaten

2 garlic cloves, minced

1 yellow onion, finely chopped

1 tablespoon Italian seasoning

¼ teaspoon kosher salt

2 tablespoons olive oil

¾ cup water, divided

8 ounces whole-wheat spaghetti, broken in half

3 cups Marinara Sauce (page 118) or store-bought marinara sauce

1. In a medium bowl, combine the beef, bread crumbs, egg, garlic, onion, Italian seasoning, and salt. Mix the ingredients together, being careful not to overwork the meat. Roll the mixture to form 16 meatballs.

2. Select Sauté on the Instant Pot and pour in the olive oil. When the oil is hot, add the meatballs and cook for 8 minutes, turning occasionally, until browned. Remove the meatballs from the pot and set aside.

3. Into the pot, pour ¼ cup of water. Scrape up any browned bits from the bottom of the pot. Press Cancel.

4. Return the meatballs to the pot and top with the spaghetti. Top the spaghetti with the remaining ½ cup of water and the marinara sauce. Do not stir. Lock the lid in place.

5. Select Manual or Pressure Cook and set the cooker to High Pressure for 3 minutes.

6. When the cook time is complete, let the pressure release naturally for 5 minutes, then quick release any remaining pressure.

7. Carefully remove the lid and stir everything together before serving.

Per serving (¼ recipe): Calories: 534; Fat: 16g; Protein: 39g; Total Carbs: 65g; Fiber: 8g; Sugar: 9g; Sodium: 295mg

Sausage and Peppers

Instead of serving sausage and peppers over pasta or on a roll, I love eating it over a nutritious bed of baby spinach. The residual heat from the sauce is enough to wilt the spinach just enough to soften and warm it though without it losing all of its texture.

SERVES 4

PREP TIME: 5 minutes

COOK SETTING: Sauté for 8 minutes, then High Pressure for 15 minutes

RELEASE: Natural

TOTAL TIME: 45 minutes

---

1 tablespoon olive oil

1 pound (6 links) Italian sausage

2 red, yellow, or orange bell peppers, seeded and sliced

1 yellow onion, sliced

1½ cups Marinara Sauce (page 118) or store-bought marinara sauce

6 cups baby spinach

1. Select Sauté on the Instant Pot and pour in the olive oil. When the oil is hot, add the sausage links and cook for 3 to 4 minutes on each side, until browned. Press Cancel.

2. Add the peppers and onion to the pot. Pour the sauce on top and do not stir. Lock the lid in place.

3. Select Manual or Pressure Cook and set the cooker to High Pressure for 15 minutes.

4. When the cook time is complete, let the pressure release naturally for 10 minutes, then quick release any remaining pressure.

5. Carefully remove the lid. Remove the sausages and slice them into rounds. Return the sliced sausages to the pot and stir to combine. Serve the sausage and peppers over the spinach.

INGREDIENT TIP: You can use chicken or pork sausage for this recipe. Whichever you choose, check the label and look for sausages made without sugar or additives, such as corn syrup, dextrose, citric acid, and "natural flavors."

Per serving (1½ sausage links and ¼ vegetable mixture): Calories: 491; Fat: 39g; Protein: 20g; Total Carbs: 16g; Fiber: 4g; Sugar: 5g; Sodium: 772mg

Pulled Pork Lettuce Wraps

Pressure cookers allow you to use leaner cuts of meat such as pork tenderloin without them drying out. A vinegary slaw adds crunch to these lettuce wraps and balances out the sweet flavor of the barbecue sauce. This recipe makes about 24 wraps.

SERVES 6

PREP TIME: 10 minutes

COOK SETTING: Sauté for 15 minutes, then High Pressure for 40 minutes

RELEASE: Natural

TOTAL TIME: 1 hour 30 minutes

2 cups coleslaw mix

¼ cup apple cider vinegar

2 tablespoons olive oil, divided

¼ teaspoon kosher salt

2 pounds pork tenderloin, cut into 4-inch cubes

1 cup water

1 cup Smoky Barbecue Sauce (page 120) or store-bought no-sugar-added barbecue sauce (labeled "paleo" or "primal")

2 heads leaf lettuce, for serving

1. In a large bowl, combine the coleslaw mix, vinegar, 1 tablespoon of olive oil, and the salt. Set aside.

2. Select Sauté on the Instant Pot and pour in the remaining 1 tablespoon of oil. Working in batches, add the pork and cook for 5 to 8 minutes, turning occasionally, until browned. Do not crowd the pot. Transfer the cooked pork to a bowl and repeat until all the pork is browned. Remove all the pork from the pot and set aside. Press Cancel.

3. Pour the water into the pot and scrape up any browned bits from the bottom. Add the barbecue sauce and return the pork to the pot. Lock the lid in place.

4. Select Manual or Pressure Cook and set the cooker to High Pressure for 40 minutes.

5. When the cook time is complete, let the pressure release naturally for 10 minutes, then quick release any remaining pressure.

6. Carefully remove the lid and shred the pork. Let the shredded pork sit uncovered in the sauce for 5 to 10 minutes to absorb more flavor. Serve the pork topped with the coleslaw and wrapped in the lettuce leaves.

Per serving (4 wraps): Calories: 274; Fat: 8g; Protein: 34g; Total Carbs: 14g; Fiber: 2g; Sugar: 9g; Sodium: 367mg

Green Curry Pork

There's nothing quite like curry to warm you up on a cold winter night. Red curry is popular, but I fell in love with green curry at one of my favorite local restaurants. Green chiles, lemongrass, and lime peel give this curry paste a bright, citrusy flavor that's less fiery than red curries. If it's still too spicy for your taste, you can tone it down by stirring a tablespoon of your favorite sweetener into the pot.

SERVES 4

PREP TIME: 5 minutes

COOK SETTING: High Pressure for 4 minutes, then Sauté for 5 minutes

RELEASE: Quick

TOTAL TIME: 20 minutes

1 (13.5-ounce) can full-fat unsweetened coconut milk

⅓ cup water

4 tablespoons green curry paste

1 pound pork tenderloin, thinly sliced

4 carrots, cut into coins

⅔ pound fresh green beans, trimmed

1 tablespoon maple syrup or coconut sugar (optional)

1. In the Instant Pot, combine the coconut milk, water, and curry paste. Mix the ingredients together until smooth. Add the pork and lock the lid in place (there's no need to mix it with the sauce).

2. Select Manual or Pressure Cook and set the cooker to High Pressure for 4 minutes.

3. When the cook time is complete, quick release the pressure. Press Cancel.

4. Carefully remove the lid and add the carrots and green beans. Press Sauté and simmer, uncovered, for 4 to 5 minutes or until the vegetables are tender. Taste the curry and stir in the maple syrup or coconut sugar (if using) before serving.

SUBSTITUTION TIP: For a vegan version of this curry, swap the pork with a large diced sweet potato and add 2 cups of fresh broccoli florets with the other vegetables in step 4. The cook time remains the same.

Per serving (¼ recipe): Calories: 381; Fat: 24g; Protein: 29g; Total Carbs: 17g; Fiber: 7g; Sugar: 5g; Sodium: 122mg

Split Pea and Ham Soup

Pea soup has seen a surge in popularity over the past few years. I have to think that at least part of that can be attributed to pressure cookers becoming more common. When made in an Instant Pot, this hearty soup can be on the table in just about 30 minutes. Pea soup will thicken as it sits, so splash in a few tablespoons of water to loosen it back up before enjoying your leftovers.

SERVES 6

PREP TIME: 10 minutes

COOK SETTING: High Pressure for 15 minutes

RELEASE: Quick

TOTAL TIME: 35 minutes

---

6 cups Chicken Stock (page 115) or store-bought low-sodium chicken stock

1½ cups dried green split peas

4 ounces sugar-free, uncured smoked ham, diced

4 carrots, diced

4 celery stalks, thinly sliced

1 leek, thinly sliced

3 garlic cloves, minced

1 tablespoon whole peppercorns

¾ teaspoon kosher salt, divided

1. In the Instant Pot, combine the stock, split peas, ham, carrots, celery, leek, garlic, peppercorns, and ½ teaspoon of salt. Lock the lid in place.

2. Select Manual or Pressure Cook and set the cooker to High Pressure for 15 minutes.

3. When the cook time is complete, quick release the pressure.

4. Carefully remove the lid and add the remaining ¼ teaspoon of salt, if necessary, before serving.

SUBSTITUTION TIP: For a vegan take on this soup, replace the ham with ¼ teaspoon of liquid smoke and use Vegetable Broth (page 116) or store-bought low-sodium vegetable broth.

Per serving (⅙ recipe): Calories: 225; Fat: 1g; Protein: 16g; Total Carbs: 39g; Fiber: 14g; Sugar: 7g; Sodium: 437mg

Braised Lamb with Apricots

Dried apricots often appear in Moroccan stews and tagines. I love how their sweet-tartness balances out the gamey lamb.

SERVES 6

PREP TIME: 10 minutes

COOK SETTING: Sauté for 8 minutes, then High Pressure for 35 minutes

RELEASE: Natural

TOTAL TIME: 1 hour 10 minutes

1 tablespoon olive oil

1½ pounds lamb stew meat, cut into 1-inch cubes

2 tablespoons balsamic vinegar

1¼ cups water

1 (15.5-ounce) can chickpeas, drained and rinsed

1 cup crushed tomatoes

½ cup unsulfured dried apricots, quartered (see Ingredient tip)

1 red onion, diced

1 lemon, thinly sliced

1 cinnamon stick

½ teaspoon kosher salt

½ teaspoon ground coriander

¼ cup fresh parsley, chopped

1. Select Sauté on the Instant Pot and pour in the olive oil. When the oil is hot, add the lamb and cook for 5 to 8 minutes, stirring occasionally, until browned. Stir in the vinegar and scrape up any browned bits from the bottom of the pot. Press Cancel.

2. Add the water, chickpeas, tomatoes, apricots, onion, lemon, cinnamon stick, salt, and coriander. Lock the lid in place.

3. Select Manual or Pressure Cook and set the cooker to High Pressure for 35 minutes.

4. When the cook time is complete, let the pressure release naturally for 10 minutes, then quick release any remaining pressure.

5. Carefully remove the lid and remove the cinnamon stick. Stir in the parsley and serve.

INGREDIENT TIP: Dried apricots are often treated with sulfur dioxide to give them a soft texture and keep their color bright. Unsulfured apricots are darker and sweeter, and they are perfect for stews like this one. Look for them in the natural foods section of your grocery store.

Per serving (⅙ recipe): Calories: 293; Fat: 10g; Protein: 28g; Total Carbs: 24g; Fiber: 5g; Sugar: 11g; Sodium: 253mg

Lamb Gyros

Traditional gyro meat is cooked on a vertical rotisserie. Thin slices of meat are shaved off and served as the meat continues to cook. Although it's nearly impossible to make authentic gyro meat at home, this meat loaf–like recipe is a close approximation. This recipe has you slice the meat thin and serve it in pita bread with yogurt-cucumber sauce, but you can also turn it into a Greek salad.

SERVES 4

PREP TIME: 15 minutes

COOK SETTING: High Pressure for 25 minutes, then Sauté for 6 minutes

RELEASE: Natural

TOTAL TIME: 1 hour

1 pound ground lamb

½ red onion,
   finely chopped

2 teaspoons dried
   marjoram

2 teaspoons dried crushed
   rosemary

2 teaspoons dried oregano

¾ teaspoon kosher
   salt, divided

1 cup full-fat plain
   Greek yogurt

1. In a medium bowl, combine the lamb, onion, marjoram, rosemary, oregano, and ½ teaspoon of salt. Press the meat mixture into a large square, about 5 inches wide and 1½ inches thick. Place the loaf on a piece of aluminum foil, then fold up the sides of the foil to catch the juices. Do not cover.

2. Pour ½ cup of water into the Instant Pot and insert the trivet. Place the foil with the lamb on top of the trivet and lock the lid in place.

3. Select Manual or Pressure Cook and set the cooker to High Pressure for 25 minutes.

4. Meanwhile, in a small bowl, combine the yogurt, vinegar, dill, and the remaining ¼ teaspoon of salt. Fold in the cucumber and set aside.

5. When the cook time is complete, let the pressure release naturally for 10 minutes, then quick release any remaining pressure. Press Cancel.

6. Carefully remove the lid and lift out the gyro meat and foil. Empty the liquid from the bottom of the pot and wipe it dry.

1 tablespoon red
  wine vinegar

2 teaspoons freshly
  chopped dill

1 small cucumber,
  shredded

1 tablespoon olive oil

4 whole wheat
  pitas, warmed

7. Return the pot to the base and press Sauté until the display reads More. Pour in the oil. When the oil is hot, add the gyro meat and cook for 3 minutes on each side, until browned. Remove the meat from the pot and slice it into very thin strips.

8. Serve the sliced gyro meat in the pitas and top them with yogurt sauce.

SUBSTITUTION TIP: Not a fan of lamb? You can also make this with lean ground beef or pork. Or try a combination of two meats.

Per serving (¼ recipe): Calories: 377; Fat: 19g; Protein: 30g; Total Carbs: 23g; Fiber: 3g; Sugar: 6g; Sodium: 438mg

Chapter 7

Desserts

Lemon Bars
PAGE 108

103

Chocolate Peanut Butter Popcorn

Although it's often thought of as a movie theater treat, popcorn is a whole grain that can make a great healthy snack when prepared without gobs of butter and salt. It's so easy to pop your own right in your Instant Pot. I dressed this version up with melty peanut butter and dark chocolate for a sweet and salty snack the whole family will love.

SERVES 4

PREP TIME: 5 minutes

COOK SETTING: Sauté for 5 minutes

RELEASE: N/A

TOTAL TIME: 10 minutes

---

1 tablespoon coconut oil

¼ cup popcorn kernels

1 tablespoon creamy
    peanut butter

2 tablespoons dairy-free
    dark chocolate chips

1. Select Sauté on the Instant Pot and pour in the coconut oil. When the oil is hot, add the popcorn kernels. When the popcorn begins to sizzle, place the lid on the pot but do not lock it.

2. Cook for 5 to 6 minutes or until the kernels stop popping on a regular basis. Press Cancel.

3. Remove the lid and stir in the peanut butter, using the heat of the pot to help it melt and coat the popcorn. Stir in the chocolate chips. Serve warm or let the chocolate set at room temperature before eating.

INGREDIENT TIP: Dark chocolate is a superfood that's rich in antioxidants and can be part of a clean eating lifestyle when enjoyed in moderation. For the best quality, look for dairy-free brands that list unsweetened chocolate as the first ingredient (brands that include dairy are generally more processed).

Per serving (¼ recipe): Calories: 140; Fat: 7g; Protein: 3g; Total Carbs: 16g; Fiber: 3g; Sugar: 2g; Sodium: 63mg

Stuffed Apples

Stuffed apples have been one of my favorite desserts ever since I learned how to make them when I was a kid at summer camp. Nuts, oats, and cinnamon combine to make a streusel-like filling that's so tasty. Use firm baking apples such as Empire, Jonagold, or honeycrisp for this recipe, because they hold their shape when cooked.

SERVES 4

PREP TIME: 10 minutes

COOK SETTING: High Pressure for 6 minutes

RELEASE: Quick

TOTAL TIME: 20 minutes

¼ cup chopped walnuts

¼ cup gluten-free
  rolled oats

3 teaspoons coconut oil

1 teaspoon maple syrup

1 teaspoon ground
  cinnamon

⅛ teaspoon salt

4 apples, cored

1. In a small bowl, combine the walnuts, oats, coconut oil, maple syrup, cinnamon, and salt. Spoon the mixture into the cored apples.

2. Pour 1 cup of water into the Instant Pot and insert the trivet. Place the apples on the trivet. Lock the lid in place.

3. Select Manual or Pressure Cook and set the cooker to High Pressure for 6 minutes.

4. When the cook time is complete, quick release the pressure.

5. Carefully remove the lid and serve the apples warm.

SUBSTITUTION TIP: Oats are naturally gluten-free but frequently become cross-contaminated with wheat in the field or during processing. If gluten is a concern for you or someone you're cooking for, be sure to buy certified gluten-free oats. Or, omit the oats altogether and increase the walnuts to ⅓ cup.

Per serving (1 apple): Calories: 197; Fat: 9g; Protein: 2g; Total Carbs: 31g; Fiber: 6g; Sugar: 20g; Sodium: 41mg

Vanilla Bean Custard

The even heat of the Instant Pot makes it perfect for cooking egg-based custards like this one. I can't get over how luxuriously creamy it is, especially since it doesn't rely on gelatin or other stabilizers. Four-ounce ramekins are perfect for individual portions. If you don't have ramekins, you can use small, pressure-safe jars, but keep in mind that they may need additional time to cook (if your custard isn't fully set, return it to pressure for another minute or two).

SERVES 4

PREP TIME: 5 minutes

COOK SETTING: High Pressure for 7 minutes

RELEASE: Natural

TOTAL TIME: 30 minutes

---

4 large egg yolks

1 cup whole milk

2 tablespoons honey

1 vanilla bean, scraped, or ¼ teaspoon vanilla extract

1. In a medium bowl, whisk together the egg yolks, milk, honey, and vanilla until smooth. Divide among four 4-ounce ramekins. Cover the tops with aluminum foil.

2. Pour 1 cup of water into the Instant Pot and insert the trivet. Place the ramekins on the trivet and lock the lid in place.

3. Select Manual or Pressure Cook and set the cooker to High Pressure for 7 minutes.

4. When the cook time is complete, let the pressure release naturally for 10 minutes, then quick release any remaining pressure.

5. Carefully remove the lid and lift out the ramekins. Serve warm or chilled.

FLAVOR BOOST: Dust the cooked custards with cinnamon or top with fresh berries.

Per serving (1 ramekin): Calories: 125; Fat: 7g; Protein: 5g; Total Carbs: 12g; Fiber: 0g; Sugar: 12g; Sodium: 35mg

Peach Cobbler

Peach cobbler is one of my ultimate comfort foods. Growing up, my mom's slow cooker version made an appearance at nearly every gathering of family or friends. Thanks to the Instant Pot, this homey dessert can now be ready in a matter of minutes. Buttermilk gives the rich biscuit topping on this cobbler a tender texture and helps it rise. If you have extra buttermilk, freeze it in 1-cup portions for up to 3 months.

SERVES 6

PREP TIME: 10 minutes

COOK SETTING: High Pressure for 10 minutes

RELEASE: Quick

TOTAL TIME: 30 minutes

1 cup spelt flour

1 tablespoon
   baking powder

2 teaspoons coconut sugar

⅛ teaspoon kosher salt

1 cup buttermilk

2 pounds frozen
   sliced peaches

¼ cup water

½ teaspoon ground
   cinnamon

¼ teaspoon ground
   coriander

1. In a medium bowl, combine the flour, baking powder, coconut sugar, and salt. Stir in the buttermilk to form a thick dough.

2. In the Instant Pot, combine the peaches, water, cinnamon, and coriander. Drop the dough, a tablespoon at a time, on top of the peaches, being careful to not let the dough touch the bottom or sides of the pot. Lock the lid in place.

3. Select Manual or Pressure Cook and set the cooker to High Pressure for 10 minutes.

4. When the cook time is complete, quick release the pressure.

5. Carefully remove the lid and let the cobbler cool for 5 to 10 minutes before serving.

SUBSTITUTION TIP: To make this recipe gluten-free, use your favorite measure-for-measure gluten-free flour blend instead of the spelt flour. To make it dairy-free, use 1 cup of coconut milk beverage (boxed, not canned) mixed with 1 tablespoon of freshly squeezed lemon juice.

Per serving (⅙ recipe): Calories: 133; Fat: 1g; Protein: 5g; Total Carbs: 29g; Fiber: 4g; Sugar: 17g; Sodium: 107mg

Lemon Bars

The lemon custard in this classic dessert is pleasantly tart, and the honey adds an additional layer of flavor. To cut these into a more traditional bar shape, slice them in a crosshatch manner; that way, the middle pieces will be rectangles and the edge pieces will only have a slight curve to them.

SERVES 6

PREP TIME: 15 minutes, plus 2 hours to chill

COOK SETTING: High Pressure for 12 minutes

RELEASE: Natural

TOTAL TIME: 2 hours 50 minutes

¾ cup gluten-free
   rolled oats
¾ cup almond flour
¼ cup melted coconut oil
2 tablespoons honey,
   plus ⅓ cup
1 teaspoon vanilla extract
¼ teaspoon kosher
   salt, divided
2 large eggs, beaten
Zest and juice of 2 lemons
1 teaspoon arrowroot
   powder or cornstarch

INGREDIENT TIP: Most of the tart flavor in these lemon bars comes from the natural oils in the lemon zest, so be sure to include it.

1. Line a 6-inch square cake pan with aluminum foil.

2. In a medium bowl, combine the oats, almond flour, coconut oil, 2 tablespoons of honey, the vanilla, and ⅛ teaspoon of salt to form a stiff dough. Press the dough into the bottom of the prepared pan.

3. In a separate bowl, whisk together the eggs, lemon zest and juice, arrowroot powder, ⅓ cup of honey, and the remaining ⅛ teaspoon of salt. Pour the mixture over the crust. Cover the pan with foil.

4. Pour 1 cup of water into the Instant Pot and insert the trivet. Place the pan on top of the trivet and lock the lid in place.

5. Select Manual or Pressure Cook and set the cooker to High Pressure for 12 minutes.

6. When the cook time is complete, let the pressure release naturally for 15 minutes, then quick release any remaining pressure.

7. Carefully remove the lid and lift out the pan. Chill the lemon bars in the refrigerator for at least 2 hours before slicing them into six portions and serving.

Per serving (1 bar): Calories: 291; Fat: 17g; Protein: 6g; Total Carbs: 31g; Fiber: 3g; Sugar: 21g; Sodium: 77mg

Carrot and Date Cake

To prevent cakes from coming out soggy, cover the pan with a paper towel before wrapping it in aluminum foil. The towel traps excess moisture and prevents it from "raining" back down on top of the cake.

SERVES 6

PREP TIME: 10 minutes, plus 1 hour to cool

COOK SETTING: High Pressure for 45 minutes

RELEASE: Natural

TOTAL TIME: 2 hours 10 minutes

Nonstick cooking spray

1 cup almond flour

2 teaspoons ground cinnamon

1 teaspoon baking soda

¼ teaspoon ground nutmeg

¼ teaspoon kosher salt

2 eggs, beaten

¼ cup pure maple syrup

½ teaspoon vanilla extract

1 cup (about 2 medium) shredded carrots

¼ cup (about 5) pitted and chopped dates

1. Grease a 6-inch cake pan with nonstick cooking spray. Set aside.

2. In a medium bowl, combine the almond flour, cinnamon, baking soda, nutmeg, and salt.

3. In a separate bowl, whisk together the eggs, maple syrup, and vanilla. Pour the egg mixture into the flour mixture and combine to form a batter. Fold in the carrots and dates.

4. Pour the batter into the prepared cake pan. Cover the pan with a paper towel (without letting it touch the surface of the batter) and then cover the top of the pan with foil.

5. Pour 1 cup of water into the Instant Pot and insert the trivet. Place the cake pan on top of the trivet. Lock the lid in place.

6. Select Manual or Pressure Cook and set the cooker to High Pressure for 45 minutes.

7. When the cook time is complete, let the pressure release naturally for 10 minutes, then quick release any remaining pressure.

8. Carefully remove the lid and lift out the cake pan. Remove the foil and paper towel and let the cake cool on the trivet for 1 hour. Cut the cake into six slices and serve.

Per serving (1 slice): Calories: 179; Fat: 10g; Protein: 6g; Total Carbs: 20g; Fiber: 4g; Sugar: 14g; Sodium: 301mg

Berry Almond Bundt Cake

This cake tastes great with any combination of small, fresh berries. Don't use frozen berries, which add too much moisture and can make your cake soggy.

SERVES 6

PREP TIME: 10 minutes, plus 1 hour to cool

COOK SETTING: High Pressure for 45 minutes

RELEASE: Natural

TOTAL TIME: 2 hours 10 minutes

Nonstick cooking spray

1½ cups almond flour, plus 1 tablespoon

1 teaspoon baking soda

¼ teaspoon kosher salt

2 eggs, beaten

½ cup buttermilk

¼ cup pure maple syrup

½ teaspoon pure almond extract

1 cup fresh berries

INGREDIENT TIP: Tossing the berries in almond flour keeps them from sinking to the bottom.

1. Grease a 7-inch Bundt pan with nonstick cooking spray.

2. In a medium bowl, combine 1½ cups of almond flour, the baking soda, and salt.

3. In a separate bowl, whisk together the eggs, buttermilk, maple syrup, and almond extract. Pour the egg mixture into the flour mixture and combine to form a batter.

4. In a small bowl, mix the berries with 1 tablespoon of almond flour until thoroughly coated. Fold the berry mixture into the batter.

5. Pour the batter into the prepared Bundt pan and cover the top with aluminum foil.

6. Pour 1 cup of water into the Instant Pot and insert the trivet. Place the Bundt pan on top of the trivet. Lock the lid in place.

7. Select Manual or Pressure Cook and set the cooker to High Pressure for 45 minutes.

8. When the cook time is complete, let the pressure release naturally for 10 minutes, then quick release any remaining pressure.

9. Carefully remove the lid and lift out the Bundt pan. Remove the foil and let the cake cool on the trivet for 1 hour. Cut the cake into six slices and serve.

Per serving (1 slice): Calories: 213; Fat: 14g; Protein: 8g; Total Carbs: 17g; Fiber: 4g; Sugar: 11g; Sodium: 326mg

Grain-Free Brownies

Who doesn't love a rich, chocolatey brownie? This grain-free recipe cooks up in your Instant Pot so you don't need to turn on the oven and heat up the whole house. You'll love the natural cocoa flavor and subtle sweetness provided by the maple syrup. These brownies will rise as they bake, so don't cover them too tightly, or the surface might stick to the aluminum foil. Also note, you'll want your coconut oil soft enough to mix in, but not melted.

SERVES 6

PREP TIME: 10 minutes, plus 1 hour to cool

COOK SETTING: High Pressure for 45 minutes

RELEASE: Natural

TOTAL TIME: 2 hours 15 minutes

Nonstick cooking spray

1 large egg plus 1 egg yolk

⅓ cup maple syrup

½ teaspoon vanilla extract

⅓ cup coconut oil, at room temperature

⅔ cup almond flour

3 tablespoons unsweetened cocoa powder

¼ teaspoon baking powder

¼ teaspoon kosher salt

VARIATION TIP: For more cake-like brownies, use 2 whole eggs and add ¼ teaspoon of baking soda.

1. Line a 6-inch cake pan with aluminum foil and grease it with nonstick cooking spray.

2. In a medium bowl, whisk together the egg, egg yolk, maple syrup, and vanilla. Mix in the coconut oil until smooth. Stir in the almond flour, cocoa powder, baking powder, and salt. Pour the batter into the prepared cake pan and cover it loosely with foil.

3. Pour 1 cup of water into the Instant Pot and insert the trivet. Place the cake pan on top of the trivet and lock the lid in place.

4. Select Manual or Pressure Cook and set the cooker to High Pressure for 45 minutes.

5. When the cook time is complete, let the pressure release naturally for 15 minutes, then quick release any remaining pressure.

6. Carefully remove the lid and lift out the pan. Remove the foil and let the brownies cool on the trivet for 1 hour. Cut the brownies into six portions and serve.

Per serving (1 brownie): Calories: 229; Fat: 18g; Protein: 4g; Total Carbs: 16g; Fiber: 2g; Sugar: 11g; Sodium: 112mg

Chapter 8

Sauces and Staples

Restaurant-Style Salsa
PAGE 117

113

Basic Beans

If you go through beans like we do in my house, you know how quickly those cans can add up—both in price and the space they take up in the recycling bin. A bag of dried beans, on the other hand, costs less than $2 and cooks up quickly in the pressure cooker. These beans also freeze well; I almost always have a few portions tucked away in the freezer for whenever I need them.

MAKES 6 CUPS

PREP TIME: 5 minutes

COOK SETTING: High Pressure for 35 minutes

RELEASE: Natural

TOTAL TIME: 1 hour 10 minutes

---

1 pound dried beans

4 cups Vegetable Broth (page 116) or store-bought low-sodium vegetable broth, or water

2 bay leaves

2 teaspoons olive oil

½ teaspoon kosher salt

1. In the Instant Pot, combine the dried beans, broth, bay leaves, olive oil, and salt. Lock the lid in place.

2. Select Manual or Pressure Cook and set the cooker to High Pressure for 35 minutes.

3. When the cook time is complete, let the pressure release naturally for 15 minutes, then quick release any remaining pressure.

4. Carefully remove the lid and discard the bay leaves.

INGREDIENT TIP: This basic recipe works for most types of beans, but older beans can take longer (as they age, their ability to absorb water diminishes). If the beans aren't soft enough once the pressure has been released, select Sauté and let them simmer for another 5 to 10 minutes. Soaking the beans overnight in cold water can also help ensure they soften quickly. Note: Red kidney beans must be cooked at pressure for at least 10 minutes to neutralize their natural toxins.

Per serving (½ cup): Calories: 133; Fat: 1g; Protein: 9g; Total Carbs: 23g; Fiber: 6g; Sugar: 1g; Sodium: 55mg

Chicken Stock

I have yet to find a store-bought chicken stock that comes anywhere close to the flavor and richness of this homemade version. Luckily, it's super easy to make in the Instant Pot and only takes a little over an hour. Chicken wings are easy and affordable for making stock, but if you have a leftover carcass from making roast chicken, you can use that instead.

MAKES 12 CUPS

PREP TIME: 10 minutes

COOK SETTING: High Pressure for 40 minutes

RELEASE: Natural

TOTAL TIME: 1 hour 20 minutes

3 pounds chicken wings

4 carrots, coarsely chopped

4 celery stalks, coarsely chopped

1 yellow onion, skin on, quartered

4 garlic cloves, smashed

2 bay leaves

1 teaspoon whole black peppercorns

12 cups water

1. In the Instant Pot, combine the chicken wings, carrots, celery, onion, garlic, bay leaves, peppercorns, and water. Lock the lid in place.

2. Select Manual or Pressure Cook and set the cooker to High Pressure for 40 minutes.

3. When the cook time is complete, let the pressure release naturally for 15 minutes, then quick release any remaining pressure.

4. Carefully remove the lid and strain the stock, discarding any solids. Refrigerate the stock in an airtight container for up to 4 days or freeze it for up to 6 months.

Per serving (1 cup): Calories: 15; Fat: 0g; Protein: 2g; Total Carbs: 1g; Fiber: 0g; Sugar: 0g; Sodium: 9mg

Vegetable Broth

Vegetable broth is one of my secret weapons in the kitchen. It makes a great base for soups, but it also adds extra flavor when you use it in place of water in recipes like Cilantro-Lime Brown Rice (page 40) or Basic Beans (page 114). Making it at home is cheaper than buying it prepared, and it's so easy; you don't even need to peel the vegetables! In fact, the onion skin gives this broth a gorgeous golden color.

MAKES 12 CUPS

PREP TIME: 5 minutes

COOK SETTING: High Pressure for 30 minutes

RELEASE: Quick

TOTAL TIME: 50 minutes

8 ounces white
  mushrooms

3 carrots, coarsely
  chopped

2 celery stalks,
  coarsely chopped

1 yellow onion, unpeeled
  and quartered

2 bay leaves

1 tablespoon kosher salt

½ teaspoon whole
  peppercorns

10 cups cold water

1. In the Instant Pot, combine the mushrooms, carrots, celery, onion, bay leaves, salt, peppercorns, and water. Lock the lid in place.

2. Select Manual or Pressure Cook and set the cooker to High Pressure for 30 minutes.

3. When the cook time is complete, quick release the pressure.

4. Carefully remove the lid and strain the broth, discarding the solids. Refrigerate the broth for up to 1 week or freeze it for up to 3 months.

INGREDIENT TIP: For a richer stock, select Sauté and brown the vegetables in a tablespoon of olive oil before adding the water and pressure cooking.

Per serving (1 cup): Calories: 12; Fat: 0g; Protein: 0g; Total Carbs: 3g; Fiber: 0g; Sugar: 1g; Sodium: 290mg

Restaurant-Style Salsa

When one of my college roommates told me the restaurant she worked at used canned tomatoes for their salsa, I couldn't believe it. But it makes sense: Using canned tomatoes ensures your salsa will have maximum flavor no matter what time of year you make it. As written, this simple but flavorful recipe makes a mildly spicy salsa. If you prefer it hotter, add more of your favorite hot sauce.

MAKES 4 CUPS

PREP TIME: 5 minutes, plus 1 hour to cool

COOK SETTING: High Pressure for 10 minutes

RELEASE: Natural

TOTAL TIME: 1 hour 40 minutes

1 (28-ounce) can whole peeled tomatoes

1 green bell pepper, seeded and chopped

1 sweet onion, diced

4 garlic cloves, minced

1 bunch fresh cilantro, chopped

1 tablespoon freshly squeezed lime juice

1 teaspoon hot sauce

½ teaspoon kosher salt

1. In the Instant Pot, combine the tomatoes with their juices, bell pepper, onion, and garlic. Lock the lid in place.

2. Select Manual or Pressure Cook and set the cooker to High Pressure for 10 minutes.

3. When the cook time is complete, let the pressure release naturally for 10 minutes, then quick release any remaining pressure.

4. Carefully remove the lid and stir in the cilantro, lime juice, hot sauce, and salt. Let the salsa cool for about 10 minutes, then refrigerate it for 1 hour before serving.

5. Store leftovers in an airtight container in the refrigerator for up to 5 days.

INGREDIENT TIP: For this salsa, I use a vinegar-based hot sauce with minimal ingredients, like Tabasco or Cholula.

Per serving (¼ cup): Calories: 18; Fat: 0g; Protein: 1g; Total Carbs: 4g; Fiber: 1g; Sugar: 3g; Sodium: 46mg

Marinara Sauce

Cooking sauce in the Instant Pot gives it that simmered-all-day flavor in under an hour. This is a great recipe to make in the summer, when tomatoes are at their peak. I love making a double or triple batch and storing it in my freezer to use later.

MAKES 4 CUPS

PREP TIME: 5 minutes

COOK SETTING: Sauté for 4 minutes, then High Pressure for 20 minutes

RELEASE: Quick

TOTAL TIME: 40 minutes

---

1 tablespoon olive oil

1 yellow onion, finely chopped

5 garlic cloves, minced

3 pounds plum tomatoes, quartered

½ cup Vegetable Broth (see page 116) or store-bought low-sodium vegetable broth

2 tablespoons double concentrated tomato paste

1. Select Sauté on the Instant Pot and pour in the olive oil. When the oil is hot, add the onion and garlic. Cook for 3 to 4 minutes, stirring occasionally, until softened. Press Cancel.

2. Add the tomatoes, broth, and tomato paste. Lock the lid in place.

3. Select Manual or Pressure Cook and set the cooker to High Pressure for 20 minutes.

4. When the cook time is complete, quick release the pressure.

5. Carefully remove the lid and stir, pressing down on any large pieces of tomato to break them down. For a smoother sauce, use an immersion blender to blend to your desired consistency. Refrigerate the marinara sauce for up to 1 week or freeze it for up to 3 months.

INGREDIENT TIP: Double concentrated tomato paste is reduced more than standard tomato paste, giving it a richer flavor. It's typically sold in resealable tubes rather than cans, which is convenient for storage.

Per serving (¼ cup): Calories: 29; Fat: 1g; Protein: 1g; Total Carbs: 5g; Fiber: 1g; Sugar: 3g; Sodium: 6mg

Sugar-Free Ketchup

I recently made it my personal mission to perfect homemade sugar-free ketchup. Sure, you can find it in stores, but it's expensive and not typically as clean an ingredient list as I'd prefer. I finally perfected a recipe that has all the classic ketchup flavor you love, but it's sweetened with dates.

SERVES 12

PREP TIME: 5 minutes

COOK SETTING: High Pressure for 5 minutes, then Sauté for 15 minutes

RELEASE: Quick

TOTAL TIME: 30 minutes

1 (28-ounce) can crushed tomatoes
1 yellow onion, quartered
4 pitted dates
¼ cup apple cider vinegar
¼ teaspoon paprika
¼ teaspoon garlic powder
¼ teaspoon kosher salt

1. In the Instant Pot, combine the tomatoes, onion, dates, vinegar, paprika, garlic powder, and salt. Lock the lid in place.

2. Select Manual or Pressure Cook and set the cooker to High Pressure for 5 minutes.

3. When the cook time is complete, quick release the pressure. Press Cancel.

4. Carefully remove the lid and discard the onion. Select Sauté and simmer for 15 minutes, stirring occasionally, until thickened.

5. Transfer the ketchup to an airtight container and refrigerate it for up to 2 weeks.

INGREDIENT TIP: Using canned tomatoes means you don't need to deal with pesky tomato skins and seeds. If you prefer to use fresh tomatoes, swap in 6 plum tomatoes for the canned. Blend the ketchup in a blender or food processor and pass it through a fine sieve before refrigerating.

Per serving (2 tablespoons): Calories: 33; Fat: 0g; Protein: 1g; Total Carbs: 8g; Fiber: 2g; Sugar: 5g; Sodium: 150mg

Smoky Barbecue Sauce

As with the Sugar-Free Ketchup (page 119), clean barbecue sauce can be hard to come by. Luckily, it's easy to make at home. This smoky version has become my go-to recipe. I love how flavorful it is, and it's made with basic ingredients that I almost always have on hand. It's great as a dipping sauce, or you can use it to make Pulled Pork Lettuce Wraps (page 96).

SERVES 12

PREP TIME: 5 minutes

COOK SETTING: Sauté for 4 minutes, then High Pressure for 10 minutes

RELEASE: Quick

TOTAL TIME: 25 minutes

1 tablespoon olive oil

½ red onion, finely chopped

2 garlic cloves, minced

1 cup Sugar-Free Ketchup (page 119) or store-bought no-sugar-added ketchup

⅓ cup water

⅓ cup pure maple syrup

¼ cup apple cider vinegar

2 teaspoons Dijon mustard

¼ teaspoon liquid smoke

1. Select Sauté on the Instant Pot and pour in the olive oil. When the oil is hot, add the onion and garlic. Cook for 3 to 4 minutes, stirring frequently, until softened. Press Cancel.

2. Add the ketchup, water, maple syrup, vinegar, mustard, and liquid smoke; stir to combine. Lock the lid in place.

3. Select Manual or Pressure Cook and set the cooker to High Pressure for 10 minutes.

4. When the cook time is complete, quick release the pressure.

5. Carefully remove the lid and serve. Store leftovers in an airtight container in the refrigerator for about 1 week.

INGREDIENT TIP: Liquid smoke is a natural flavoring made by condensing wood smoke. It's a great way to add a smoky, grilled flavor to your recipes. Look for it in small bottles wherever spices and extracts are sold, and use it sparingly; a little bit goes a long way.

Per serving (2 tablespoons): Calories: 42; Fat: 1g; Protein: 0g; Total Carbs: 8g; Fiber: 0g; Sugar: 6g; Sodium: 13mg

Homemade Yogurt

Why make homemade yogurt? Because it has a creamy texture and delicate, milky flavor that commercial versions can't touch. Yogurt needs to be held at a constant temperature while it incubates, so the Instant Pot is the perfect tool. There are a few steps involved, and it's a long process, but the results are worth it. Use the last scoop of your store-bought yogurt to make this recipe instead of taking another trip to the grocery store. Once you've made your first batch of homemade yogurt, you can use some of it to make your next batch.

SERVES 8

PREP TIME: 5 minutes, plus 2 hours to cool

COOK SETTING: Yogurt

RELEASE: N/A

TOTAL TIME: 10 hours 35 minutes

8 cups milk

1 tablespoon plain yogurt

1. Pour the milk into your Instant Pot. Press the Yogurt button until the display reads BOIL. Heat the milk, stirring occasionally, for about 30 minutes, until it reaches 180°F on a kitchen thermometer. Press Cancel.

2. Fill your sink with a few inches of cold water. Remove the inner pot from the Instant Pot and place it directly into the sink. Stir vigorously for about 5 minutes, until the milk cools to 110°F.

3. In a small bowl, combine ¼ cup of hot milk with the yogurt. Whisk the ingredients together until smooth, then stir it back into the pot of milk. Wipe the outside of the pot dry and place it back in the Instant Pot. Lock the lid in place.

4. Press the Yogurt button until the display reads 8:00.

CONTINUED

5. When the time expires, remove the lid and give the pot a gentle shake. The yogurt inside should move together as one mass.

6. For thick, Greek-style yogurt, strain it through a cheesecloth. For traditional yogurt, no straining is required. For both versions, refrigerate the yogurt for at least 2 hours, until cooled, then stir. Note that the yogurt will get a little thinner as it combines with the whey at the bottom of the pot.

FLAVOR BOOST: To make yogurt parfaits, stir in 1 teaspoon of vanilla extract, then layer each serving with your favorite fresh fruit or 2 tablespoons of fruit preserves.

Per serving (½ cup): Calories: 150; Fat: 8g; Protein: 8g; Total Carbs: 12g; Fiber: 0g; Sugar: 11g; Sodium: 106mg

Measurement Conversions

VOLUME EQUIVALENTS	U.S. STANDARD	U.S. STANDARD (ounces)	METRIC (approximate)
LIQUID	2 tablespoons	1 fl. oz.	30 mL
	¼ cup	2 fl. oz.	60 mL
	½ cup	4 fl. oz.	120 mL
	1 cup	8 fl. oz.	240 mL
	1½ cups	12 fl. oz.	355 mL
	2 cups or 1 pint	16 fl. oz.	475 mL
	4 cups or 1 quart	32 fl. oz.	1 L
	1 gallon	128 fl. oz.	4 L
DRY	⅛ teaspoon		0.5 mL
	¼ teaspoon		1 mL
	½ teaspoon		2 mL
	¾ teaspoon		4 mL
	1 teaspoon		5 mL
	1 tablespoon		15 mL
	¼ cup		59 mL
	⅓ cup		79 mL
	½ cup		118 mL
	⅔ cup		156 mL
	¾ cup		177 mL
	1 cup		235 mL
	2 cups or 1 pint		475 mL
	3 cups		700 mL
	4 cups or 1 quart		1 L
	½ gallon		2 L
	1 gallon		4 L

OVEN TEMPERATURES

FAHRENHEIT	CELSIUS (approximate)
250°F	120°C
300°F	150°C
325°F	165°C
350°F	180°C
375°F	190°C
400°F	200°C
425°F	220°C
450°F	230°C

WEIGHT EQUIVALENTS

U.S. STANDARD	METRIC (approximate)
½ ounce	15 g
1 ounce	30 g
2 ounces	60 g
4 ounces	115 g
8 ounces	225 g
12 ounces	340 g
16 ounces or 1 pound	455 g

Resources

"Clean 15" and "Dirty Dozen"
The Environmental Working Group's annual "Clean 15" and "Dirty Dozen" lists can help you prioritize your spending on organic versus conventional produce. (EWG.org/foodnews)

Instant Pot User Manuals
If you misplaced the manual that came with your Instant Pot, you can download a new one. (InstantPot.com/english-manuals)

Clean Eating Magazine
This is a great source for tasty clean eating recipes. (CleanEatingMag.com)

Bob's Red Mill
My go-to brand for whole grains and gluten-free flours.

Tessemae's
High-quality organic salad dressings and condiments brand.

Primal Kitchen
My favorite unsweetened ketchup and barbecue sauce brand.

Index

H

About the Author

Lauren Keating is the author behind the blog *Healthy Delicious*, where she has shared easy weeknight recipes made with fresh, nutritious ingredients for over a decade.

Lauren studied plant-based professional cooking through Rouxbe cooking school and uses those skills to incorporate fruits, vegetables, and whole grains into her recipes in unique ways.

Lauren lives in Upstate New York with her husband, Shawn, and their two dogs. She lives by the motto: If it isn't delicious, it isn't worth eating.

Find more healthy inspiration from Lauren's first two books, *Healthy Eating One-Pot Cookbook* and *Healthy Meal Prep Slow Cooker Cookbook*, or dive into the world of pressure cooking in her *Instant Pot Cookbook for Beginners*.

CPSIA information can be obtained
at www.ICGtesting.com
Printed in the USA
BVHW020125280821
615029BV00002B/3

9 781648 764554